Drive and Stroll

Surrey

David Weller

COUNTRYSIDE BOOKS
NEWBURY BERKSHIRE

First published 2005
© David Weller, 2005

COUNTRYSIDE BOOKS
3 Catherine Road
Newbury, Berkshire

To view our complete range of books,
please visit us at
www. countrysidebooks co.uk

ISBN 1 85306 905 1

Cover picture of Shere supplied by Derek Forss

Photographs by the author
Designed by Peter Davies, Nautilus Design

Produced through MRM Associates Ltd., Reading
Typeset by Jean Cussons Typesetting, Diss, Norfolk
Printed by Arrowsmith, Bristol

Contents

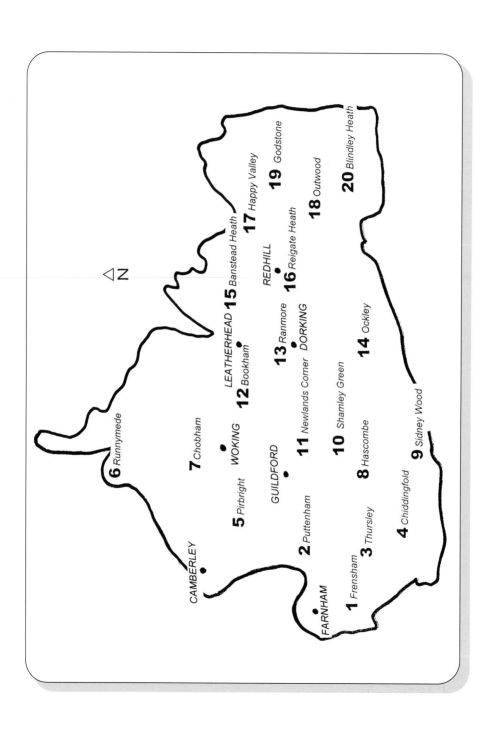

Contents

PUBLISHER'S NOTE

We hope that you obtain considerable enjoyment from this book; great care has been taken in its preparation. Although at the time of publication all routes followed public rights of way or permitted paths, diversion orders can be made and permissions withdrawn.

We cannot, of course, be held responsible for such diversion orders and any inaccuracies in the text which result from these or any other changes to the routes nor any damage which might result from walkers trespassing on private property. We are anxious, though, that all details covering the walks are kept up to date and would therefore welcome information from readers which would be relevant to future editions.

The simple sketch maps that accompany the walks in this book are based on notes made by the author whilst checking out the routes on the ground. However, for the benefit of a proper map, we do recommend that you purchase the relevant Ordnance Survey sheet covering your walk; the sheet number of the OS Landranger series is given at the beginning of each chapter. Ordnance Survey maps are widely available, especially through booksellers and local newsagents.

Introduction

What a great idea on a lovely summer's day – pack up a simple picnic, drive to a picturesque spot and enjoy a short stroll where you can fill your lungs with fresh air and feast your eyes on the wonderful Surrey countryside. All the routes in this book are circular, easy to follow and pass through scenery that varies from wildflower meadows, heaths draped in purple heather, pine-scented woodland and alongside the shimmering waters of lakes, brooks and streams. If you have young children with you or don't wish to embark on a longer more energetic walk, then this is the book for you. All in all, I think that these great circuits will enchant you no matter what time of year you try them.

The sketch maps are drawn to scale and contain numbers that correspond with each numbered paragraph in the text. To get the most out of the walk, though, I do recommend you also carry the relevant OS map which will give you a greater overview of the circuit. All the starting points are easy to find and for those who prefer not to carry a picnic, I have supplied details of a recommended eatery along or near each route together with its telephone number so that you may make arrangements in advance.

Within each walk instruction are points of interest that you will pass along the way, whether it be an old windmill, an historic building or rare wildflowers – I hasten to add, please don't pick any wildflowers – they always look much better where they are and even the most common may have taken many years to establish.

I would recommend you wear stout walking shoes or boots as the ground underfoot might be a little uneven or slippery. A useful item, I find, is a small haversack containing a flask of coffee or a cold drink for when a pretty spot is chanced upon and you wish to sit awhile to admire the view or watch the wildlife.

I hope you will gain the same pleasure in following these lovely circuits as I did in devising them.

David Weller

1 Frensham Common and Great Pond

The visitor centre at Frensham Great Pond

The Walk 2¾ miles **Terrain** Level with one small hill
Map OS Landranger 186 Aldershot & Guildford (GR 844403)

How to get there

From the A31 at Farnham take the A287 south for 3 miles to reach Frensham village. Continue south and turn right 50 yards after passing the village green and school. **Parking**: The signed Frensham Great Pond free car park will be found to your left in ½ mile (open 9am–9pm).

Drive and Stroll

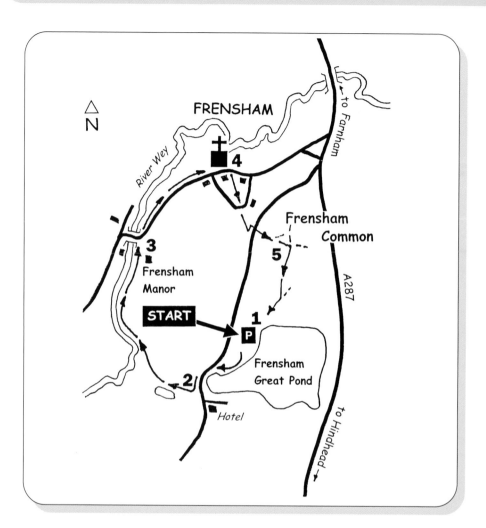

Introduction

This very pleasant stroll begins by the shore of Frensham Great Pond before soon following the gently flowing waters of the River Wey south branch. Peace and tranquillity prevail as the level path passes between trees that line its bank and you may even see the turquoise blue flash of a kingfisher going about its business. The path ends at the site of an old water mill and from here a short stroll along a country lane brings you to St Mary's church.

The route continues past pretty cottages and turns towards Frensham Great Pond via a track romantically named Lovers' Lane which brings you to

Frensham Common where easy sandy paths lead through pine trees and finally bring you back to the car park and the Information Centre where there is a small display explaining the flora and fauna of the area.

The Holly Bush

Frensham village is split in two – the core of the old village is centred around the 13th-century church that is passed on the stroll, and the other by the cricket pitch in Shotfield Road ½ mile to the north and it is here that you will find the Holly Bush. This pleasant pub offers a good selection of food that ranges from toasted sandwiches, jacket potatoes and ploughman's lunches to main courses that include a lemon sole with parsley sauce dish. Telephone: 01252 793593.

    Frensham Great Pond Visitor Centre, next to the car park, is open during the summer months, and serves both hot and cold snacks and drinks.

THE WALK

From the car park go towards the fine expanse of water and turn right on a path that traces the shore. Remain close to the water's edge and when a lane is met, continue on the lane following the shoreline leftwards.

Frensham Great Pond and Little Pond (not seen on this route) are enlarged natural pools that were created as stew ponds in the 13th-century to help feed the household of the Bishop of Winchester who resided at Farnham Castle. During the Second World War they were drained to stop them from being a navigational aid to enemy bombers attacking Aldershot. Very quickly trees began to grow on the dry lakebeds and many locals believed they would never see the fine expanse of water again. Soon after the war ended sterling efforts were made to clear the new growth and the ponds were restored to their former glory.

Soon at roadside railings, turn right on a signed bridleway. After passing a peaceful pond on your left the bank of the **River Wey south branch** is met and the route continues alongside its gently flowing waters. Later ignore a footbridge on your left and continue alongside the river to reach the site of an old watermill by a country lane.

Maintain direction ahead along this peaceful lane and enjoy the fine views it offers over the surrounding countryside. After ½ mile a cluster of cottages and **St Mary's church** are met.

Drive and Stroll

The sandy shore of Frensham Great Pond

Inside St Mary's church is an enormous copper cauldron of great age that is said to have once belonged to Mother Ludlam, a benevolent witch who lived in a cave at Moor Park. Aubrey wrote in the 17th century that it was 'brought here by the fairies' and used for their feasts. Salmon, another Surrey historian, wrote in 1736 that it was filled with ale and used 'for the entertainment of the village at the wedding of poor maids'. Aubrey must have been supping the ale if he believed his version!

 (4)

90 yards after passing the church turn right into **Lovers' Lane** and when this soon ends press on along a well-trodden footpath. Cross a residential road and continue ahead on a footpath to reach a second road. Here turn left along the road for 30 yards before turning right on a signed footpath that leads uphill between trees.

 (5)

When nearing the top of the incline, ignore a left fork and keep ahead to meet a T-junction with a broad track. Turn right here and follow the well-defined path as it descends the ridge to meet a wide crossing track. Turn right now and follow the horse ride back to the car park and the end of this peaceful circuit.

Place of Interest Nearby

The Rural Life Centre and Old Kiln Museum, just to the north-east of Frensham, contains a large collection of farm machinery, carts, wagons and ploughs. Open Wednesday to Sunday and Bank Holiday Monday between April and October from 10am to 5pm; November to March Wednesday and Sunday only 11am to 4pm. Telephone: 01252 715571.

2 | Around Puttenham Common

A sandy track across Puttenham Common

The Walk 3¼ miles **Terrain** Sandy paths across undulating heath
Map OS Landranger 186 Aldershot & Guildford (GR 920461)

How to get there

Puttenham is 3 miles west of Guildford. Turn south off the A31 and follow the signs to reach Puttenham in ½ mile. **Parking**: From Puttenham's main street, turn left on a lane opposite the Good Intent pub to reach Puttenham Common top car park in 1½ miles.

Drive and Stroll

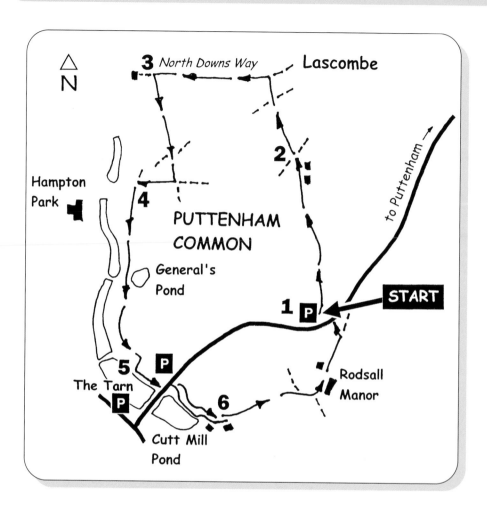

Introduction

This stroll is around the scenic heathland of Puttenham Common where the panoramic views are quite stunning. Beginning beside a large picnic area, the circuit meets a wide track that passes through woodland to reach a section of the North Downs Way. Turning west along this pleasant track the path goes down to reach a woodland dell where it turns southwards on a slowly rising path that brings you to the site of an ancient hill fort and Puttenham Common's highest point.

From here the circuit descends easily through more pleasant woodland and passes by General's Pond to reach The Tarn, a wonderful lake with interesting water birds that include heron and great crested grebe. After following the water's edge for a short while the way continues alongside the bank of picturesque Cutt Mill pond before passing the mellow stonework of Rodsall Manor and returning to the car park and the end of this lovely stroll.

The Good Intent.

Puttenham village lies under the southern chalk slopes of the Hog's Back where you can still see hops growing for the local brewing industry. Along the main street near the church is the Good Intent pub, a hostelry that has welcomed travellers since the 16th century and is still popular with those passing the door whilst walking the North Downs Way long distance path. As well as supplying real ales, the pub offers good, simple fare from a varied bar menu every lunchtime and during the evenings from Tuesday to Saturday, with fish and chips a speciality on Wednesday evenings which you can either eat in or take away. Telephone: 01483 810387.

THE WALK

From the large car park, follow a line of short posts along the left side of the picnic area. Some 20 yards after entering woodland at a slight dip, turn right to meet a track. Now turn left and remain on this track until it ends at a junction of footpaths.

At this junction of paths press on ahead along a bridleway that begins by following a small line of power cables and goes up a rise to reach an open area of heath with far reaching views. Go over a crossing path and carry on to reach a T-junction by a line of low posts. Turn left now on this downhill path that forms a section of the **North Downs Way**.

At a small parking area at the foot of the slope where a cottage is seen through the trees ahead, turn left between posts on a bridleway. Soon bear right at a fork and now keep to this bridleway as it gradually gains height to finally meet a wide crossing track on open heath. This open area with its great views makes the perfect picnic spot. Now turn right on the sloping crossing track and ignore a crossing path in a dip to soon reach a T-junction with a barbed-wire fence ahead of you.

Turn left on this downhill path that skirts the grounds of **Hampton Park**. As the path reaches the foot of the slope it leads you past **General's Pond**, a peaceful woodland pool. Keep to the main path and after going down a dip and crossing a tiny brook, the path forks by a post. Here go right to meet the bank of **The Tarn** and another fine picnic spot.

Strung out like pearls amongst the bracken and trees are six wonderful pools. The Tarn is the biggest and it is worth staying awhile to watch the water birds go about their daily business. As well as heron and mallard, the great crested grebe lives here and you may well be treated to the sight of their unique head-bowing courtship dance.

Turn left along the bank of the lake to reach a road. Cross to the driveway of **Cutt Mill House** opposite and ignore all the private signs, as the drive is a public bridleway and a right of way. Follow the drive past the picturesque lake and keep to it as it winds its way past the entrance to **Cutt Mill House**. Follow the drive past **Garden Cottage** and after passing **Willow Cottage** press on ahead along the right-hand side of a garage to reach woodland.

Picturesque Rose Cottage

The bridleway continues ahead through the woodland to reach the driveway to **Rodsall Manor**. Turn right along the curving drive and keep right at a fork to pass close by the manor house, which was built as far back as 1680. Press on ahead and continue to the right of a stone built barn to pass lovely 18th-century **Rose Cottage**. The path now continues ahead and in 80 yards you should fork left and continue between steep banks. In 150 yards look out for a marker post to your left where you should turn left up a stepped path where, after passing a house you reach the entrance to **Puttenham Common**'s top car park and the end of this fine stroll.

Place of Interest Nearby

The Hog's Back Brewery is a working, independent brewery sited in a building dating back some 250 years. A brewery tour shows the making of their 24 ales in progress. Open all year on Mondays and Tuesdays from 10am to 6pm; Wednesday to Friday 10am to 8.30pm; Saturday from 9am to 8.30pm and Sunday from 10.30am to 4.30pm. Manor Farm, The Street, Tongham, Farnham. Telephone: 01252 783000.

3 Around Thursley Common and Bog

Thor's Stone, an ancient boundary marker

The Walk 2½ miles **Terrain** Level paths and boardwalks through the bog that require small children to be kept in check.
Map OS Landranger 186 Aldershot & Guildford (GR 899416)

How to get there

Thursley Common is easiest reached from Elstead. Take the B3001 from the A3, 4 miles south of Guildford. At Elstead's tiny village green, turn left into Thursley Road. **Parking**: The Moat free car park will be reached on your left after 1¼ miles.

Drive and Stroll

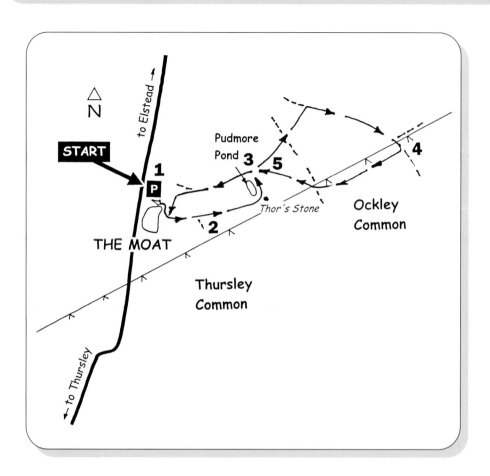

Introduction

This stroll is perfect for budding naturalists. The circuit begins beside The Moat, a wonderfully picturesque pond teeming with wildlife and home to the rare raft spider. As the way leaves the water's edge it meets a boardwalk that leads you through Thursley Bog, a vestige of wetland habitat that has become so rare in England. It is worth taking binoculars with you, as this is the place to see many rare birds, plants and over 20 species of dragonfly that live here.

After leaving the boardwalk and passing the end of Pudmore Pond, a wetland pool, the circuit meets with a wide path that takes you around Ockley Common which is ablaze with colour in late August when the heather is in flower. The figure-of-eight route returns past Pudmore Pond on a wide bridleway and all too soon ends back at The Moat, which makes a great picnic spot.

The Pride of the Valley Hotel

Just 2½ miles south-west of The Moat car park at the corner of Jumps Road and Tilford Road is the impressive Pride of the Valley Hotel. As you will notice by the signage outside, this was Lloyd George's local and if it was good enough for him then it should be good enough for us. There is a wide selection of food from the bar and à la carte menus. I particularly enjoyed a double baked Stilton soufflé with salad and mixed nut dressing from the 'Lighter Bites' menu. Telephone: 01428 605799.

THE WALK

The unique mixture of wet heath, bog pools, sphagnum moss and, in the dryer areas Scots pine and heather, makes this place one of the best examples of its kind in the south of England.

 (1)

From the car park walk towards the bank of **The Moat** and turn left on a path that remains close to the water's edge. Five yards after the path turns away from the pond, turn right at a small junction of paths. At another junction of paths in 30 yards, turn left to soon meet an **English Nature Reserve** signboard. Here ignore a crossing track and continue ahead where the path joins a boarded walkway.

Take your time now as you follow this walkway for there is plenty to see. In the small pools are water boatmen while dragonfly continually patrol the surface. Overhead fly woodlark, nightjar, Dartford warbler and hobby while another species always seen here is the 'twitcher'. During early summer marsh orchids will be seen in flower from the boardwalk whilst all around are the tiny sundew, Britain's only insectivorous plant. When I passed this way one sunny August day, dozens of baby lizards were sunning themselves on the boardwalks.

 (2)

Later ignore a boardwalk to your right and continue ahead to reach **Pudmore Pond**. Here the path makes a left turn and continues along a line of Scots pine to reach a wide crossing path.

Just to the right-hand side of the boardwalk by Pudmore Pond is Thor's Stone, used as a boundary marker as far back as the year 909 in the reign of Edward the Elder. Although there is no doubt that it was used as a boundary marker it is questionable as to whether its name isn't just a romantic 19th-century attachment dreamt up by local Victorian author Baring-Gold in his novel The Broom Squire.

  (3)

Turn right now along the wide path ignoring side paths as you enter trees. Soon ignore a crossing track and keep ahead as you pass between tall pines to reach a T-junction with a wide cart track. Ignore a path opposite and turn right along the cart track.

The Moat – a wonderful picnic spot

  (4)

Follow this pleasant track until it turns sharply left under power cables, ignore a path ahead and turn right on a path that remains parallel to the cables. This narrows and passes through trees before going between gorse bushes to reach a small junction of paths. Ignore a path to your right and press on ahead on one that now swings to the right and passes under power cables. The path crosses an open area of the bog before ending at a wide crossing path.

 (5)

Turn left here and remain on this path until a fork is met. Follow the left-hand sandy track to meet a T-junction. Turn left and in 70 yards meet the **English Nature Reserve** signboard. Now turn right and retrace your steps back to **The Moat** and the end of this interesting circuit.

Place of Interest Nearby

The Packhorse Antique Centre is jammed full of interesting paraphernalia and makes a fascinating place to visit even if you don't buy the odd bargain. There is also a very pleasant cafeteria. Open from 10.30am to 5.30pm 7 days a week (no dogs). Tongham Road, 2 miles west of Puttenham. Follow the brown tourist signs from the A31. Telephone: 01252 781010.

4 Chiddingfold and The Downs

Chiddingfold pond and church

The Walk 3¼ miles **Terrain** Slightly undulating with one hill
Map OS Landranger 186 Aldershot & Guildford (GR 961354)

How to get there

From the Milford roundabout 4½ miles south of Guildford, follow the A283 Petworth Road for 5 miles to reach Chiddingfold and its village green. **Parking**: Around the village green.

Drive and Stroll

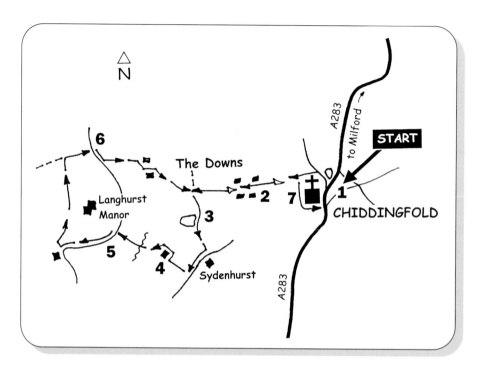

Introduction

This charming circuit starts from beside Chiddingfold's picturesque village green and within yards passes a lily-covered pond. Soon the route negotiates the only hill of note on the circuit, as the way climbs to a lofty piece of countryside known as The Downs. There are lovely views from this vantage point and the way now levels and passes along a quiet road before joining up with pretty fields. As the circuit turns southwards it passes through a woodland dell and alongside a scenic pool amongst the trees.

After following a short stretch of quiet country lane, the route swings back towards Chiddingfold and passes through newly planted woodland and open fields by Langhurst Manor. Imperceptibly the heights of The Downs are rejoined, and, with great views over the surrounding countryside the circuit meets up with its outward path that is now followed back to Chiddingfold and the end of the stroll.

The Crown Inn

Dating back to 1285 when a guesthouse stood on the site, the Crown Inn has documentary evidence of the present building dating from 1383 and so it lays claim to be the oldest pub in Britain. Sited at the southernmost point of Chiddingfold's village green, the inn makes for a splendid place to take nourishment. Lunchtime offerings vary from a selection of sandwiches and lighter dishes that include a mouth-watering mozzarella, grilled vegetables and green basil pesto dish, while a good selection of main courses include cod fillet in Badger ale batter and an olive branch fish pie dish. As well as a good selection of beers from the bar, tea, coffee, cappuccino and espresso are also available. Telephone: 01428 682255.

THE WALK

1

The village green has seen many people and events in its time – the huge annual bonfire, fetes and fairs, but nothing to match the time when 15-year-old King Edward VI stayed overnight at the Crown Inn in 1552. His retinue numbered 4,000, most of whom camped out on the green.

Make your way to the southernmost end of the village green and cross the **A283**. Now continue along the lane beside the lily-covered pond and when it soon bends right, turn left on a signed footpath. Continue through a kissing gate and press on ahead on a rising tarmac path that passes a graveyard. Although fairly steep, it soon levels and brings you to a quiet residential road dotted with a few well-spaced houses.

 ### 2

Continue ahead along the road and when it bends right, go ahead on a fenced path beside the gate to a house named **The Downs**. The short path brings you to a field with lovely views and you should continue ahead along its top edge. In 180 yards look out for a stile to the right under an oak tree. Do not cross the stile, but turn left here on an indistinct downhill path that brings you to woodland.

 ### 3

Continue through a woodland dell where you pass by a peaceful woodland pool. Press on ahead and through a gate beside a garage and continue along a driveway to reach a country lane. Turn right along the lane and when opposite a wonderful barn conversion, turn right along a cart track that leads to **Blackhams** and **Sydenhurst** farms.

 ### 4

Some 30 yards before the cart track ends at a gateway turn right for 35 yards before turning left and continuing alongside a garden fence with a pretty cottage displaying wonderful herringbone brickwork beyond. In 20 yards, after passing a gateway, turn left over a stile and keep ahead and pass through a kissing gate at the edge of woodland. Now cross a bridge over

The path across the fields

a woodland stream, bear slightly left and continue ahead through woodland between low banks to reach a country lane.

 (5)

Turn left along the lane until it bends leftwards by a large house named **Hawlands**. Here turn right on a farm track and in 70 yards turn right through a field gate and press on through a wonderful planting of young trees of great variety. The grassy path brings you to stile at a field edge. Keep ahead here alongside the grounds to **Langhurst Manor** and when the fence turns

away to the right, keep ahead across the open field. Aim for a group of oak trees 120 yards to the left of a barn seen ahead and pass through a kissing gate on your right. Now follow a lovely tree-lined path, soon ignoring a stile on your left to reach a lane.

 (6)

Turn right along the lane and look out for a stile to your left 40 yards after passing the entrance to **Langhurst Manor**. Cross the stile and continue through a field in the direction of an idyllic cottage at its far end. As you near the cottage, follow the indistinct path rightwards and cross a stile. Turn right to meet a driveway and turn left to very soon meet a gateway. Here go through a gate on your left and continue on a footpath that skirts a garden. Pass through a kissing gate and in 20 yards cross a stile to enter a large field. Continue ahead on a path that follows the left-hand edge to rejoin the outward route. Remain ahead now and retrace your steps back to **Chiddingfold**.

  (7)

Along the way you may wish to vary your route slightly by turning right at the graveyard and following a path between the graves to pass **St Mary's church** where you continue through the lych gate with its unique coffin rest and rejoin **Chiddingfold's** village green.

A woodland pool

In days gone by when pallbearers carried the coffin directly from the deceased's home to the church, they placed it in the lych gate to await the priest and the rest of the mourners. The roof gave shelter from inclement weather and a seat gave rest to the bearers. Generally lych gates contain a wide seat on either side for this purpose but in this case the coffin rest is central. A short service was often held here prior to the funeral service proper within the church. The word 'lych' is Old English for corpse.

Place of Interest Nearby

Ramster Gardens are set in 20 acres of mature woodland; the gardens are planted with azaleas, rhododendrons and camellias that are especially colourful in spring and early summer. Open from the end of April to the end of July between 11am and 5pm. South of Chiddingfold on the A283. Telephone: 01428 654167.

Drive and Stroll

5 Around Pirbright

The village green and pond at Pirbright

The Walk 3 miles **Terrain** Easy level paths
Map OS Landranger 186 Aldershot & Guildford (GR 947559)

How to get there

Pirbright is on the A324, 4 miles north of Guildford. When travelling north, turn right by the Moorhen pub. **Parking**: Park in the lay-by beside the village pond. Further parking can be found around the green.

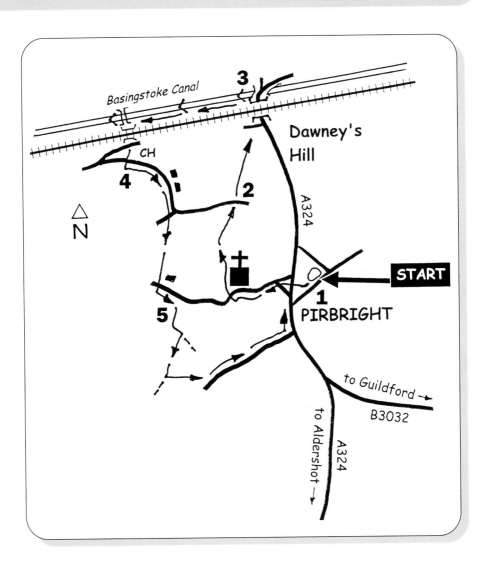

Introduction

This easy and varied stroll takes in quiet country lanes, shady woodland paths and the restored towpath of the Basingstoke Canal. After leaving Pirbright's lovely village green the way continues past the graveyard of St Michael's church where its most famous memorial is marked by a large granite monolith inscribed 'Bula Matari' – the African name for the famous writer and traveller, Sir Henry Morton Stanley.

Drive and Stroll

Seeking out a shady path beside the church, the circuit continues through woodland to meet the towpath of the Basingstoke Canal where the tree-lined path makes a pretty scene as the arching trees overhead are reflected in the still waters. Soon it is time to leave this magical place and the route turns back towards Pirbright. After following another woodland path the way continues over pretty meadows to reach a quiet lane that brings you back to the village green to complete the stroll.

The Moorhen

What is it that started the modern trend of renaming pubs I wonder? For years this lovely establishment was called the White Hart – so long, in fact, that a part of the village green is officially named White Hart Corner – never mind, your visit here will always be enjoyable. The eatery is open from 12 noon until late in the evening and serves sandwiches (until 5pm), light meals like Irish mussels in saffron and white wine and main courses that include minted lamb cutlets. Telephone: 01483 799715.

THE WALK

(1)

Leave the village pond and cross the large green to meet the **A324**. Continue over the **A324** and cross a triangle of grass to reach **Church Lane** where you should continue ahead.

Just over the low wall surrounding St Michael's graveyard there is a large granite monolith marking Sir Henry Morton Stanley's grave. This is the same Stanley who uttered those immortal words 'Doctor Livingstone I presume'. His wish was to be buried in Westminster Abbey next to Livingstone but this was refused. The inscription 'Bula Matari' is the name given him by his African porters and means 'rock breaker'.

Continue along the lane to reach **St Michael's church**. Turn right here and cross a brook and continue on a woodland path that passes to the left of the church.

(2)

When a road is reached, cross it diagonally to the right and press on ahead along another woodland path to reach a second road. Go ahead here with caution, as there is no footpath, and pass under the railway bridge to meet the towpath of the **Basingstoke Canal** to your left in 50 yards.

The Basingstoke Canal contains 29 locks, 69 bridges, a tunnel and 2 aqueducts in its 37-mile route from Weybridge to Basingstoke. As canal traffic in general declined, its last gasp came during the 1850s when it

26

St Michael's church

delivered building materials to the extensive army barracks in the area. After falling into disrepair and becoming not much more than a muddy ditch in places, hundreds of volunteers, plus the combined efforts of Hampshire and Surrey Councils came together in 1973 and after 20 years' hard work have revived the canal to what you see today.

 ③

Now press on along this very pleasant towpath until you meet **Cowshot Bridge**. Here turn left under the railway to meet a road. Cross the road to the entrance gates of **Goal Farm golf course** and follow a path to the right of the gates to soon reach a quiet country lane.

 ④

Turn left and, after passing some houses, go ahead on a narrow path when the lane turns sharply left. Very soon cross a road and continue ahead on a path through trees to reach **West Heath Cottages** that proudly proclaim a building date of 1880. Keep ahead to meet and follow a tarmac lane past the end of **Thompsons Close** to reach a country lane.

Drive and Stroll

The Basingstoke Canal

  (5)

Turn left along the lane and turn right on a footpath 35 yards after passing the entrance gate of **The Old School House**. After crossing a brook the path swings left and meets a kissing gate at a field edge. Here go diagonally right on an indistinct path that climbs a knoll topped by trees to meet a second kissing gate. Pass through the gate and turn left downhill to pass through a third kissing gate under a spreading oak tree. Keep ahead along a field edge to reach a quiet lane. Turn left along the lane and follow it back to the **A324** where another left turn brings you back to **Pirbright** village green.

Place of Interest Nearby

The Royal Logistic Corps Museum in The Princess Royal Barracks at Deepcut displays artefacts ranging from the 14th century to the present day. Open all year from Tuesday to Friday from 10am to 4pm. Despite the address, the museum is outside the barracks on the B3015 northwest of Pirbright. Telephone: 01252 833371.

6 Runnymede and Langham's Pond

The Magna Carta memorial at Runnymede

The Walk 2¾ miles **Terrain** Level with one small hill
Map OS Landranger 176 West London (GR 008724)

How to get there

Runnymede Pleasure Grounds are off the A308 ½ mile north-west of Egham and junction 13 of the M25. **Parking**: There is a pay and display car park.

Drive and Stroll

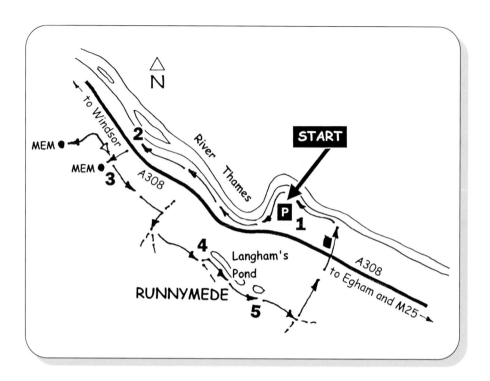

Introduction

This fascinating stroll through history is combined with acres of spring and summer wildflowers in quantities unparalleled elsewhere in Surrey. Beginning at the popular Runnymede Pleasure Grounds that are a delight for the picnicker, the circuit follows the bank of the River Thames before heading for the serene Magna Carta Memorial. From here there is a short diversion that leads you up a granite path between trees to visit the peaceful John F. Kennedy Memorial.

Soon the way makes for the famous water meadows and joins the bank of scenic Langham's Pond that abounds with wildlife. After following the water's edge for a short distance, the path continues through magnificent meadows that are covered with tall grasses and myriads of wildflowers. Near the end of the circuit, the route returns to the bank of the Thames where you soon rejoin the Pleasure Grounds. The circuit is through water meadows and is best left for the drier spring and summer months.

Runnymede Cafeteria.

Near the entrance of the car park and within the Pleasure Grounds is the pleasant little Runnymede Cafeteria. With tables outside under an all-weather covering, the café offers simple sustenance that ranges from sandwiches, baguettes, jumbo sausage hot dogs, tea, coffee, cold drinks and ice cream, making it a handy place to relax and enjoy a snack.

THE WALK

From the pay and display car park head for the **River Thames** that borders the picnic area and turn left along its bank. You will notice over to your left, high amongst the trees of **Cooper's Hill**, the fine building of the **Commonwealth Air Forces Memorial**, which makes an interesting place to visit. Continue alongside the river until finally you are opposite the domed **Magna Carta Memorial** to your left.

The Magna Carta Memorial was built by the American Bar Association and was paid for by voluntary contributions from American lawyers. It was unveiled in July 1957 at a ceremony attended by both British and American lawyers.

Now turn left and cross the **A308** and press on over a meadow to reach the gate of the memorial grounds. A short and not to be missed diversion rightwards here brings you to the foot of a cobbled granite path that contains 60,000 setts. Follow this path uphill between the trees to soon reach the **John F Kennedy Memorial** and a little piece of America. Now retrace your way back down the path where quite eerily the steps vanish in front of your eyes. When back at the **Magna Carta Memorial** pass by the gate and continue ahead to meet two stiles.

It was here, in these water meadows that King John was brought to book on 15th June 1215, when to quell an uprising by his powerful barons, he signed an agreement brokered by Stephen Langton, Archbishop of Canterbury. The document, known as Magna Carta – Latin for Great Charter, laid down some basic human rights for his subjects and so started the beginning of English law that was to spread throughout the world.

Ignore the right-hand stile and cross the one in front of you and maintain direction ahead along the right side of a meadow to meet a directional sign to the **Air Forces Memorial**. Turn right here through a kissing

The River Thames at Runnymede

gate and soon pass through two others to meet woodland and a **Cooper's Hill Wood** information board by a junction of paths. Turn left now and continue to the left of a stepped path. The path remains just within woodland and after 50 yards at a fork, keep left to reach a crossing path by a marker post. Turn left over a stile and then go diagonally right over a meadow to reach the bank of **Langham's Pond**.

The 12 acres of rich flora and fauna at Langham's Pond make

it a Site of Special Scientific Interest. The 'ox-bow' pond was formed from a meander of the Thames that was eventually by-passed many centuries ago when the river changed its course.

  (4)

Ignore a stile to your left and continue rightwards alongside the peaceful water. Cross a stile ahead of you and keep ahead alongside the pond and at its end, turn left through a kissing gate and continue ahead ignoring a planked path to your left. Now maintain direction on an indistinct path through a wonderful wildflower meadow and after passing a small pool you should follow the path as it swings rightwards and brings you to a kissing gate.

The unimproved meadows here abound in several types of grass as well as oxeye daisy, lesser knapweed, sorrel, buttercup, and small groups of ragged robin, a flower characteristic of water meadows but becoming increasingly rare in Surrey.

 5

Ignore the gate and bear left along the edge of a large meadow. After passing over a small bridge keep ahead to reach a directional post. Turn left now on a path through the grasses and ignore all side paths to finally reach the **A308** main road. Cross a stile and press on over the road and continue ahead alongside a bleak looking storage facility to rejoin the **River Thames**. Turn left here to very soon rejoin the **Runnymede Pleasure Ground**.

Place of Interest Nearby

The **Commonwealth Air Forces Memorial** on Cooper's Hill commemorates the 20,401 airmen and women who were killed in the Second World War and who have no known grave. The lovely design of the memorial echoes that of an airfield control tower and there are great views across the Thames from the 'observation room'. Signed from the A328 at Englefield Green. Telephone: 01784 432891.

7 | Around Chobham Common

A wide track across Chobham Common

The Walk 4 miles **Terrain** Level sandy paths
Map OS Landranger 186 Aldershot & Guildford (GR 995635)

How to get there

Gracious Pond Road is best reached from Stonehill Road that links the B386 at Addlestone to the A319 just east of Chobham. **Parking**: Park in the Chobham Common Fishpool Car Park in Gracious Pond Road.

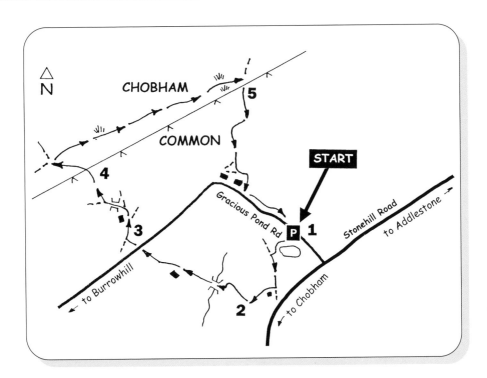

Introduction

This most enjoyable stroll begins beside a lily-covered pool amongst tall pines where there is a good chance of spotting grey heron fishing at its margins. The way then continues through varied and interesting scenery before bringing you to the sandy paths of wonderful Chobham Common, a Site of Special Scientific Interest. This magical place boasts many rare species of birds and insects and is the last of its kind in the south-east of England and a rarity in Europe.

Wide paths offer you far-reaching views over the common and take you past heathland pools where rare flowers grow and dragonflies patrol the water's surface while overhead there is always a chance to see visiting birds going about their business. After following a wide track through the south-eastern part of the common, the route makes its return through stands of pine before meeting Gracious Pond Road, where just a short stroll along this quiet and pretty lane brings you back to the car park to complete the circuit.

Drive and Stroll

The Four Horseshoes

This is a particular favourite of mine on a hot summer's day as you can sit in the shade of an umbrella at a table on the patio facing a small green. The pub serves simple bar food in ample quantities as well as a good selection of thirst-quenching beers. To find the Four Horseshoes, continue along Gracious Pond Road away from Stonehill Road to eventually reach a T-junction with the B383 at Burrowhill. The pub will be seen ahead and to the right across the green. Telephone: 01276 857581.

THE WALK

From the car park, head away from **Gracious Pond Road** on a path with exposed tree roots to reach the bank of a beautiful pool.

This surprisingly is not Gracious Pond, that lies off the route on private land and is a small nature reserve managed by Surrey Wildlife Trust and closed to the public.

Follow the bank rightwards and 30 yards after crossing a small sluice at a shady corner of the pond turn right on a well-trodden path between posts to meet a T-junction in 20 yards. Turn left along this bridleway for 60 yards before pressing on ahead on a narrower path when the bridleway bends sharply left. Cross a stile on your right 100 yards before a road is met and continue ahead alongside a field edge with buildings close to your left. Pass a solitary beech tree to reach a marker post at the edge of woodland.

Do not enter the woodland but remain in the field and turn right along the woodland edge. As the woodland ends, turn left and in 50 yards go right and cross a wooden bridge over a stream. Now press on ahead on a waymarked path across fields towards a line of trees where you go over a stile under an oak tree to meet a farm drive. Now continue ahead along the drive to reach a road.

Cross the road and continue along the driveway to **Langshot Equestrian Centre**. In 90 yards turn right between low posts and continue along a bridleway. Keep left at a fork in 30 yards and keep left again at a second fork. Remain on this path as it keeps within the woodland edge. Some 110 yards after crossing a bridge over a stream fork right alongside a ditch on your right to meet a crossing track in 20 yards. Go ahead here on a wide track and soon fork right as the path now leads you onto **Chobham Common** proper and towards power cables.

The pond at the beginning of the walk

The 1,450 acres of the common is the largest National Nature Reserve in the south of England and one of the finest of its kind in Europe. Owned by Surrey County Council, the reserve is managed by Surrey Wildlife Trust Countryside Services, a great combination that ensures that the welfare of the common and its wildlife is paramount.

  (4)

Continue under the power cables to meet a wide junction of tracks. Turn right now and continue for 1 mile along a wide undulating sandy track that remains parallel to the power cables and ignore all side paths.

When I came this way one hot June day I was privileged to be able to watch a roe deer and her young fawn grazing just to the side of the path. Later, where the path passes a small heathland pool an orchid was in flower while the tiny insectivorous sundew, no more than 1cm high, displayed its spoon-shaped leaves edged with sticky hairs that glistened in the sun.

Drive and Stroll

The vast expanse of Chobham Common

↰ (5)

After passing between wetland areas with wooden railings each side of the path, go ahead to meet a marker post at a junction of tracks. Now turn right and in 30 yards keep to the left fork on a slowly rising track that passes under the power cables. Remain on this well-used track at all times as it winds its way around the common. Keep left at a fork when the path finally narrows and goes between trees with woodland to your left. At a T-junction in 20 yards turn left and follow the bridleway as it skirts two gardens to meet **Gracious Pond Road**. Now an easy stroll leftwards along the quiet lane brings you back to the car park and the end of this lovely circuit.

Place of Interest Nearby

Brooklands Museum
If you are into old cars and aeroplanes then this place is for you. Open Tuesday to Sunday all year plus Bank Holidays, the museum is 5 miles east of Chobham in Brooklands Road, Weybridge. Telephone: 01932 857381.

8 Around Hascombe

Making friends at the beginning of the walk

The Walk 3¾ miles **Terrain** Undulating but none too taxing
Map OS Landranger 186 Aldershot & Guildford (GR 997398)

How to get there

Hascombe sits on the B2130 3½ miles south-east of Godalming. When travelling from Godalming, look out for Mare Lane on your right in the centre of Hascombe village, signposted to the village hall. **Parking**: Park at the roadside.

Drive and Stroll

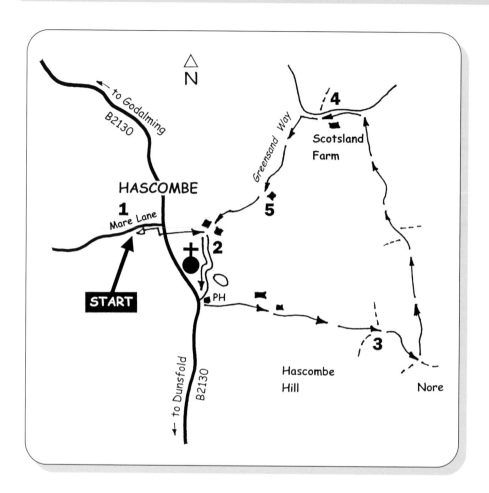

Introduction

This easy-to-follow stroll is through some of the most glorious rural scenery Surrey has to offer. Starting off near Hascombe village hall, the circuit soon crosses a small stream and passes by a cluster of rose-adorned cottages facing an idyllic pond. After passing the door of the White Horse pub, the circuit meets a rising scenic path that offers wide views over the countryside. Having crossed a ridge, the way turns north along a wonderful mile-long track where there are superb views over fields to Leith Hill in the distance.

Another turning point comes when beside lovely Scotsland Farm – a little piece of heaven amongst the trees, and it is here that the route now follows the Greensand Way long-distance path through woodland that offers fine shade on a hot summer's day and all too soon the circuit brings you back to Hascombe.

The White Horse

Situated at the southern end of the village and in a conservation area, the White Horse pub is well known to those walking the Greensand Way that passes the door. The food is highly recommended and there is plenty to choose from, including a good range of sandwiches, huge ploughman's lunches and cooked meals such as a mouth-watering asparagus and sun-dried tomato risotto dish. Telephone: 01483 208258.

THE WALK

(1)

From **Mare Lane** walk back to the **B2130** and turn right and within yards meet an interesting water fountain.

Try the clear spring water yourself, the villagers do, and can often be seen filling their drinking water bottles from it.

From the fountain cross the road to a path opposite and continue alongside **Fountain Cottage** and its garden. Cross a stream and at a bridleway press on ahead to reach **Lower House**, a pretty house built of local stone with courses of galleting.

Many of the houses in these parts are built of local stone that is of irregular shape, which in turn leads to wide joints in the mortar leaving an inherent weakness. To overcome this and to add strength to the mortar, small stones are inserted into each course, a process known as 'galleting'.

 ### (2)

Turn right along this peaceful lane and soon pass a pretty pond to reach the **White Horse** pub. Immediately after passing the pub turn left on a bridleway along a drive leading to **Hascombe Place Farm**. Keep ahead and when by the entrance of a splendid Georgian house, maintain direction ahead through a gate and pass to the right of a cottage. Now keep ahead on the path as it climbs easily to the top of a ridge.

 ### (3)

At the top of the ridge ignore side paths and continue ahead on a downhill path that is heavily eroded. At a T-junction beside a tennis court, turn left and in 15 yards by a gate turn left again along a track. Remain on this wonderful track for the next mile and enjoy the fantastic views it offers. When the track finally ends at a quiet lane, you should turn left along it.

Superb views along the way

Pass by lovely **Scotsland Farm** where parts of the building date as far back as the 15th-century and where, during spring the rhododendrons and azaleas display themselves admirably. At the end of the garden turn left on the signed **Greensand Way**. Now follow the blue **GW** arrowed signs as the path zigzags uphill to a barn.

Pass the barn and in 50 yards fork right on a bridleway that goes downhill between banks to reach a house. Press on ahead and pass between stone gateposts to reach **Lower House** where you should now turn right and retrace your steps remembering to fork left on the narrower path before crossing the stream and meeting with the road. Be careful here as the path ends rather unexpectedly at the roadside. Turn right and in a few yards meet **Mare Lane** and the end of this excellent stroll.

Place of Interest Nearby

Winkworth Arboretum at Hascombe Road, Godalming, is a marvellous woodland hillside, planted with over 1,000 different trees and shrubs that bring springtime colour from the azaleas and stunning autumn golds from the maples. Dogs are welcome on leads. Open daily until dusk. Telephone: 01483 208477.

9 Around Sidney Wood

Wide tracks lead through the woodland

The Walk 3½ miles **Terrain** Level woodland tracks and field paths
Map OS Landranger 186 Aldershot & Guildford, Camberley & Haslemere
(GR 026351)

How to get there

Sidney Wood is 1 mile west of the A281 on a lane that links Alfold
Crossways to Dunsfold. **Parking**: The car park at Sidney Wood.

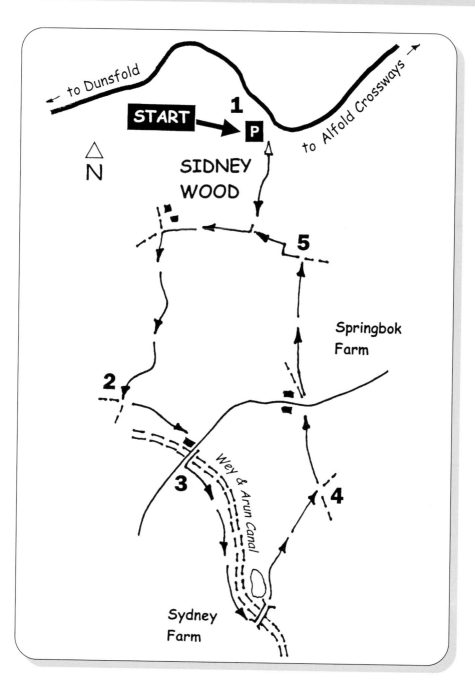

to Dunsfold

START

1 P

to Alfold Crossways

N

SIDNEY WOOD

5

Springbok Farm

2

Wey & Arun Canal

3

4

Sydney Farm

Introduction

This magnificent stroll is through fine indigenous woodland that once formed a part of the great forest covering the Surrey and Sussex Weald. The route leads you along quiet tracks lined with springtime wildflowers while birdsong seemingly resounds from every tree. Within yards of leaving the car park, you are immersed into this woodland wonderland and the hustle and bustle of modern-day living is left far behind.

Heading for the Sussex border along wide level tracks the circuit eventually joins a remnant of the Wey & Arun Canal that cuts through here. Known as London's lost route to the sea, sterling efforts are being made by a small band of volunteers from the Wey & Arun Canal Trust to restore sections of the defunct canal. As the way leaves the towpath it crosses a couple of fields that are in Sussex before rejoining the woodland and Surrey. The stroll is eminently suitable for hot summer days when shade is required but can become sticky underfoot during winter months.

The Sun Inn

Just a mile west along the road from the car park is the village green of Dunsfold where the Sun Inn and a warm welcome await. With a lovely enclosed garden for summer days and two roaring log fires to keep you snug and warm in winter, it is the ideal place to take on sustenance. There is a good selection of sensibly priced snacks and main dishes from the menu and it is always worth keeping an eye on the chef's specials board for that something different. Telephone: 01483 200242.

THE WALK

Sidney Wood lies in the 'fold' country and together with Chiddingfold, Alfold, Dunsfold and Ifold was the centre of the 13th-century glass making trade. The woodland is named after the de Sydenie family from nearby Alfold and, quite remarkably, so is Sidney in Australia.

From the car park go out to the track you came in on and turn right along it heading away from the road and deeper into **Sidney Wood**. When the path meets a T-junction, turn right along the wide track. Soon after passing equestrian paddocks to your right, another T-junction is met. Here turn left along the wide track. Unseen through the trees to your right are the remains of the defunct **Wey & Arun Canal**. Small patches of **wild strawberry** grow in the low grasses and if you pass at the right time you may like to sample their sweet fruit – of course you will

Drive and Stroll

The towpath of the defunct Wey & Arun Canal

have to beat the rabbits to them first. Remain on this lovely track until after rounding a left bend, it meets with a wide crossing path.

 (2)

Turn left here and continue along the wide track until it passes through a gate and close by a house and meets a country lane. Turn right along the lane for 30 yards before turning left along what was once the canal's towpath.

The 5-mile section of canal through Sidney Wood from Compasses

Bridge to Loxwood required 11 locks to cope with the 90-foot ascent. One mile west of here was the Wey & Arun Canal Company's main workshop that maintained this part of the canal as well as building lock gates and barges for sections further afield. The workshop still survives as a fine private residence.

 (3)

Continue along the towpath until a wooden bridge is met. Turn left over the bridge and enter a field. Now follow the path around the edge of a woodland pool and go through a gate to meet and cross a stile under an oak tree. Entering **Sussex** now you should go ahead through the centre of this field and aim towards an oak tree on the left of a line ahead of you. Cross a stile just beyond it and continue along the left-hand field edge to reach a fingerpost in its top left corner.

 4

Turn left through a gate and continue along the top edge of a field on a waymarked bridleway to reach woodland. Continue ahead through the woodland as the route rejoins **Surrey**. Cross a country lane and continue ahead on the bridleway. In a few yards, seek out a narrower path 10 yards to your right. The path initially shadows the bridleway and you should remain on it ignoring the occasional side path. The path finally ends at a T-junction with a field ahead of you through the trees.

 5

Turn left now and in 150 yards, at a junction of wide tracks, turn right for 8 yards before turning left and maintaining your direction along a wide forest track. When the wide track that you walked earlier is met on your right, turn right along it to arrive back at the car park.

Place of Interest Nearby

Smithbrook Kilns is a unique shopping centre in the middle of the countryside. Sited on the A281 north of Alfold it has a restaurant, coffee shop, craft workshops and a variety of small shops selling anything from antique clocks, fabrics and jewellery through to scuba diving equipment. There is free parking and it is open during normal business hours.

10 Shamley Green and Run Common

The duck pond at Shamley Green

The Walk 4 miles **Terrain** Level with one hill
Map OS Landranger 186 Aldershot & Guildford (GR 033437)

How to get there

Shamley Green sits on the B2128 4 miles south of Guildford. When travelling from that direction, turn left a few yards after passing the Red Lion Inn. **Parking**: Park alongside the road by the village pond.

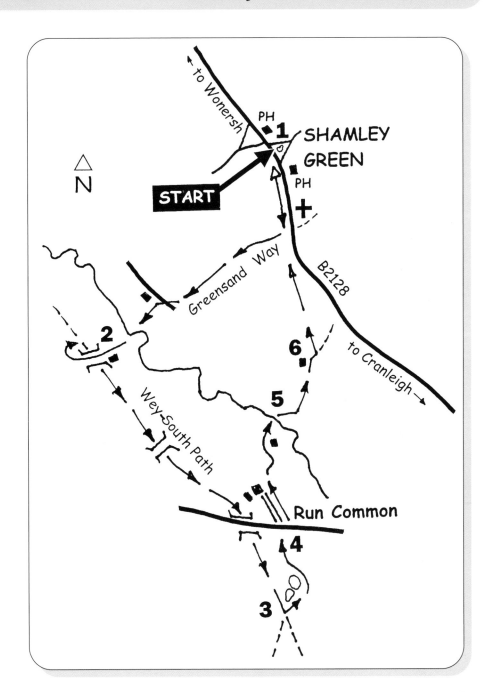

Drive and Stroll

Introduction

This glorious circuit has everything – village pond, lovely rural views, picnic spots and easy walking along well-defined paths and tracks. Leaving the village green behind, the way soon immerses itself within a rural idyll with wonderful views over a wide shallow valley. After crossing a small river, the route meets up with the Wey-South Path that utilises the old track bed of a railway that suffered the same fate as the Wey & Arun Canal that it conspired to topple. Over recent years this wonderful long-distance path has become a linear haven for wildlife.

   As the route swings back towards Shamley Green it passes by a couple of woodland pools before following the towpath of a short section of the canal across Run Common. Leaving the canal behind, the circuit winds its way between open fields with good views and all too soon brings you back to the village green.

The Red Lion Inn

With tables set out on the pretty village green during summer, this lovely pub makes for a very pleasant place to stop and enjoy good ales and plentiful food. The small bar serves traditional ales and snacks while in the comfortable restaurant you can order dishes that include duck in blackcurrant sauce, fish pie and the local favourite of sausage and mash. Children's portions and vegetarian dishes are also available. Booking for the restaurant is essential during summer weekends. Telephone: 01428 606565.

THE WALK

From the duck pond, walk south across the green towards the **Bricklayers Arms** pub. Continue along the right-hand side of the **B2128** road and a few yards after passing a church ignore a footpath ahead of you and turn right along a **Greensand Way** signed bridleway.

Once known as Shamble Lea, the village seems not to have featured much in history although it is recorded that Oliver Cromwell granted a charter for an annual fair to be held.

Follow the well-defined path between fields to reach a quiet lane. Here go diagonally right over the lane and continue along a waymarked path. Pass through a gate and continue down a slope to soon cross a small river. Now go diagonally right and pass through a gate in the top right corner of a field.

Run Common, Wey & Arun Canal

 2

Go ahead along a cart track and pass **Fanesbridge Cottage**. Immediately after passing the parapet of a bridge, turn right down steps to meet the **Wey-South Path**. Now turn right along the straight level path that once formed the track bed of a railway. This offers easy walking, but be aware that it is also a cycle route. Continue along the level path that in springtime is lined with wild flowers and pass under two further bridges. Close by to your left are the indistinct remains of the old canal.

 3

After passing under the second bridge look out for a small piece of woodland on your left. At the woodland's end, turn left on a narrow path and go through a kissing gate. Continue past a couple of woodland pools, at the end of which the path swings leftwards and continues between trees. At a small meadow, turn right along its edge to very soon meet a road.

 4

Cross the road and continue along the right-hand side of the defunct canal.

Drive and Stroll

This small section of the Wey & Arun Canal is the only reminder that Run Common was once an industrial site and not as peaceful as it is today. During the 1840s Richard Medland ran a canal-side furnace that burnt 2,000 tons of wood annually in the manufacture of naphtha, acetic acid and charcoal, most of which was transported to London by barge. During some winters the works were brought to a standstill when ice prevented the wood-laden barges from reaching the furnace.

This short section of the canal ends abruptly by a pretty house and you should now turn right along a signed footpath that follows a cart track. Keep to the cart track as it winds its way between fields. Soon after passing an isolated field bower, pass through a gate and continue ahead and cross a bridge over the river.

 5

Immediately turn diagonally right across the corner of a field and go towards a couple of field gates. Continue through the left-hand gate and follow a rising path alongside a ribbon of trees that, during springtime is lined with bluebells and the windflower. When the gates of a house are met, continue along the drive and after 70 yards go left over a stile to enter a field.

 6

Now follow the right-hand field edge to meet a marker post at the corner of woodland. From here maintain your direction across the rising field and when at its brow, head for the top right corner by a road. Continue ahead and retrace your steps back along the road to return to the village green.

Place of Interest Nearby

Dapdune Wharf on the Wey Navigation in Guildford was once a boat-building yard. Now restored, the wharf offers interactive exhibitions, children's activities and boat trips. There is also a riverside picnic area. It is open from the end of March to the end of October on Thursdays from 12 noon to 5pm and on Saturdays, Sundays and Bank Holiday Mondays from 11am until 5pm. Telephone: 01483 561389.

11

Newlands Corner and St Martha's Hill

St Martha's church is situated on the Pilgrim's Way

The Walk 4¼ miles **Terrain** Undulating with two energetic hills
Map OS Landranger 186 Aldershot & Guildford (GR 043491)

How to get there

Newlands Corner is on the A25 and 1½ miles south of West Clandon.
Parking: There is a free car park.

Drive and Stroll

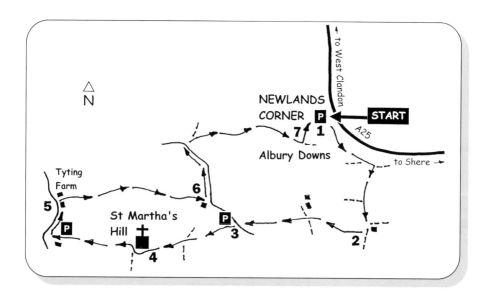

Introduction

This circuit must rate as one of the best short walks in Surrey, but beware – it is not for the faint-hearted although if you pace yourself it is easily achievable and more than worth the extra effort required. As you descend from the heights of Newlands Corner, the route immediately treats you to glorious views across Albury Downs and from the foot of the hill it follows paths that lead you through farmland where the scenery is quite superb.

Just before the halfway point the way leads you over the wonderful pine and heather-draped slopes of St Martha's Hill where the fairly stiff climb to the church is rewarded by breathtaking views from the summit. After descending from this lovely place, the circuit returns along a peaceful track that brings you back to the slopes of the downs where panoramic views across Surrey are to be seen as you stroll over open grassland to reach Newlands Corner and the end of this cracking walk.

The Barn Restaurant and Coffee Shop

Handily placed opposite Newlands Corner car park entrance, this good little eatery has tables set out in a pleasant garden during the summer months. Home cooked food from a varied menu will please all tastes. The restaurant opens at 8am on weekdays and 9am at weekends for hearty breakfasts and then continues to serve lunches and cream teas throughout the day. Telephone: 01483 222820.

Car Park Snack Bar Burger and chips, muffins, salad rolls, ice creams as well as hot and cold drinks are available from the snack bar in the car park during daylight hours.

THE WALK

Local tradition has it that Newlands Corner is named after Abraham Newland, chief cashier of the Bank of England whose name appeared on bank notes for thirty years from 1778 but that doesn't quite explain how the name appears on Bowen's map of 1749 when Abraham would have been an unknown young lad. It is in fact named after an earlier Abraham Newland who owned nearby Postford Mill.

Walk back towards the entrance of the car park where to the right you will see a post signing the **North Downs Way**. Ignore the direction indicated and go rightwards on a downhill stony track. As you near the foot of the slope woodland begins to close in and you should ignore a path to your right, but 40 yards later at a second world war pillbox, turn right along an eroded track between banks. Soon the way meets a farm track and you should continue following this. Keep ahead when a farm track comes in from your right but soon look out for a junction of bridleways by cottages high on a bank to your left.

Turn right here on an uphill path

with a bluebell wood to your left and superb views towards **Newlands Corner** on your right. Soon pass through a gate and press on along a well-trodden path across a field to reach a second gate. Press on ahead now on the fenced path until a quiet lane is reached.

Cross the lane and continue on the signed path opposite to reach a small parking area. Now bear left on a path signed as a self-guided trail. Keep ahead as the sandy path rises and follows a line of posts that separate the bridleway from the footpath. Ignore side paths and remain ahead on the broad uphill path to eventually reach **St Martha's church**.

St Martha's is thought to be a corruption of St Martyrs and, situated as it is on the Pilgrim's Way, was visited by those travelling to Canterbury to pay homage.

The route follows the graveyard wall leftwards where some welcome seats are passed. When a gate is reached at the far side of the church, go left on a wide downhill track that you should remain on until you eventually pass a vehicle barrier and reach a driveway. Turn right along the drive to soon join a road where you continue ahead to a left bend by a cottage.

  5

Turn right here on a bridleway and pass between the buildings of **Tyting Farm**. Remain ahead on this lovely track as it leads you through the valley floor to eventually reach a lonely cottage in an idyllic setting some 20 yards before reaching a country lane.

Looking towards Newlands Corner

 6

Turn left when opposite the cottage and follow a well-trodden path that remains parallel to the lane. The path ends at steps that lead down to the lane and you should continue opposite on the signed **North Downs Way**. In 20 yards keep right at a fork and continue along the **North Downs Way** as it emerges onto open downland. Remain ahead along the top of the slope with woodland close to your left and wonderful views to your right where below, almost the entire route of the stroll can be traced.

Small groups of cowslips grow amongst the short grasses on the hillside here in spring and early summer. It is a sad fact that this once abundant wildflower used in herb medicine as a sedative, is now becoming quite rare in Surrey.

 7

As you near **Newlands Corner** follow a well-trodden path that bears left up a slope to meet the car park and the end of this truly magnificent route.

Place of Interest Nearby

The Silent Pool one mile east along the A25 at Sherbourne Farm has entered into local folklore via the writings of Martin Tupper who lived in Albury. It was he who wrote the purely fictional Victorian novel, *Stephan Langton* where a fair maid and her brother were drowned in the clear waters of the chalk spring as they tried to escape from the evil King John. It is open all year round.

12 Around Little and Great Bookham Commons

A woodland path

The Walk 2¼ miles **Terrain** Level and easy
Map OS Landranger 187 Dorking, Reigate & Crawley (GR 125558)

How to get there

From the A246, 2 miles west of Leatherhead town centre, turn into the High Street at Great Bookham. At its end continue ahead along Church Lane and pass Bookham railway station. **Parking**: Turn right into The Approach, signposted to Bookham Grange Hotel, and after 200 yards you will meet the parking area at a bend.

Drive and Stroll

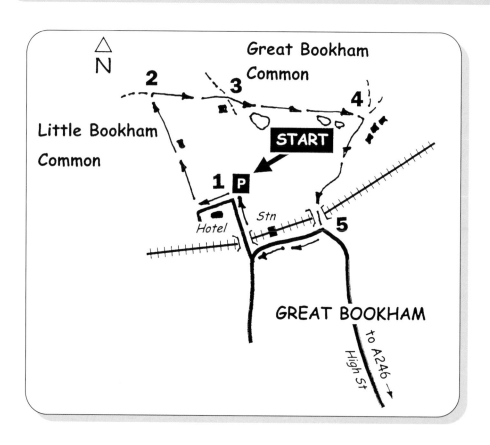

Introduction

This easy-to-follow stroll takes you through the magnificent woodland of Little and Great Bookham Commons. Although tiny rivulets cut through the area and form woodland pools, the circuit is suitable for all weathers as, for most of its way, it follows hard-surfaced paths. Attracted by the damp woodland and secluded pools, the area is alive with wildlife and makes for an interesting place to visit.

Along the way the circuit passes one of the larger pools on Great Bookham Common that makes a great place to picnic. With birdsong ringing from the trees overhead and well-placed seats at the water's edge, what more could you ask for? Soon after passing a couple of smaller pools, the route begins to head back along another hard-surfaced path between the trees and before long Bookham railway station is passed and the end of the stroll is all too soon.

Scoulers

Sited at number 27 in Great Bookham's narrow High Street is this great little eatery with a couple of sunny tables set out on the pavement where you will find service with a smile. Most food is home-cooked and includes quiches and speciality meats. If these don't tempt you, then try the home-made fish cakes, fresh filled baguettes, hot oven-baked potatoes and made-to-order sandwiches. Their cakes are made with free-range eggs and ingredients that have no preservatives, the most popular being lemon drizzle cake. To quench your thirst are organic juices, cappuccino and speciality teas. Telephone: 01372 467066.

THE WALK

(1)

Ignore a couple of paths at the parking area and continue alongside the road where you soon pass **Bookham Grange Hotel**. Immediately after passing the hotel, turn right on a tarmac drive where you pass by allotments. Remain ahead along the cart track and after passing a couple of remote cottages, cross a cattle grid to meet with a junction of bridleways in 20 yards.

Both Little and Great Bookham commons formed a part of the Saxon settlement called Bocham, meaning 'the village by the beeches'. In 1923, local residents clubbed together and bought Great Bookham Common and donated it to the National Trust. A year later they kindly did the same for Little Bookham Common thus saving this lovely area for the nation.

 (2)

Turn right here on a bridleway that leads you between the trees of **Little Bookham Common**. Ignore side paths and remain on the hard-surfaced path until it meets with a crossing bridleway. Turn right here to reach a small parking area on your right with **Merritt's Cottage** beyond.

 (3)

The way continues ahead along the well-trodden bridleway that is signposted to **Fetcham**. Follow this lovely path as it crosses **Great Bookham Common** and passes several woodland pools, the first within yards of the parking area. This pool makes a good picnic site and has a few well-sited seats for you to enjoy. The ducks are extremely friendly so it is worth bringing something for them also.

 (4)

When this straight path meets with a junction of tracks with housing beyond, turn right along a path to soon meet with a tarmac track at the end of houses. Press on ahead

One of several woodland pools

between the trees on a tarmac path to finally reach another parking area with a road beyond.

Continue ahead to meet the road and turn right along it where you soon pass by **Bookham railway station**. Turn right into the lane signpost to **Bookham Grange Hotel** to reach the parking area and the end of the walk.

Place of Interest Nearby

Polesden Lacey is signposted off the A246 ¼ mile west of Great Bookham's High Street. The Regency villa is one of the National Trust's premier houses in Surrey and is open from the end of March to the beginning of November, Wednesday to Sunday from 11am to 5pm. The walled rose garden, lawns, gift shop and tearoom are open throughout the year from 11am to 6pm or dusk. Telephone: 01372 452048.

13 | Ranmore and Polesden Lacey

Lovely scenery along the way

The Walk 4½ miles **Terrain** Wide tracks through undulating scenery.
Map OS Landranger 187 Dorking, Reigate & Crawley (GR 142503)

How to get there

From the A24 by Dorking Station head west along Ashcombe Road. At its end turn right into Ranmore Road. **Parking**: The National Trust pay and display car park is at the crest of the hill on Ranmore Common.

Drive and Stroll

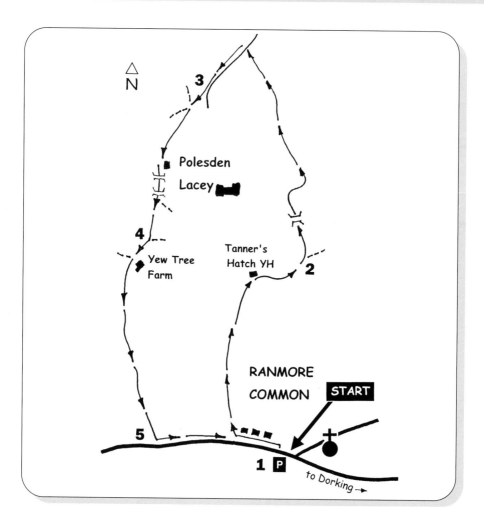

Introduction

With plenty of picnic spots along the way, this magnificent circuit is easily followed and passes through scenery unsurpassed in the south-east. Starting off from beside Steer's Field with its panoramic views over Dorking, the route soon enters the cool shade of mature beech woodland where it follows a cart track to reach isolated Tanner's Hatch Youth Hostel that sits in an enviable setting. After reaching the valley floor the track gains height easily and passes through the lovely parkland of Polesden Lacey where, on a clear day, there are views as far as the city of London.

As the route circumnavigates the National Trust grounds of Polesden Lacey, it makes its return by re-crossing the valley on another fine track through scenic countryside before entering majestic woodland. A lovely cart track now leads you easily through the dappled shade of the woodland and brings you to Ranmore where it is just a short stroll to the car park and the completion of this great circuit.

Denbies Wine Estate

As well as the extensive vineyard, the estate has two rather nice restaurants. The Conservatory Restaurant is open all year round and offers sandwiches and soups plus hot and cold dishes that can be consumed at tables surrounded by exotic plants. The more stylish Gallery Restaurant is for the over 18s where light lunches are served. Telephone: 01306 734661.

THE WALK

There is no village of Ranmore – it could hardly be described as a hamlet, just a few cottages set back from the road, so the explanation of the magnificent St Barnabus church in Ranmore Common Road must lie elsewhere. Built in 1859 by Sir George Gilbert Scott for the first Lord Ashcombe, the wonderful cobbled church has a spire more befitting a cathedral. Lord Ashcombe lived at nearby Denbies House – now demolished, and was the son of Thomas Cubitt, builder of grand houses and a huge fortune.

 1

From the car park go back to the road (it's probably safer to cross to the wide grassy area opposite) and turn left. Remain parallel to the road until you reach the wonderfully tiled walls of **Rose Cottages**. Turn right

here on a cart track that passes to the left of the cottages and signed to **Tanner's Hatch Youth Hostel**. Keep to this lovely downhill track through woodland for 1 mile and remain on it as it swings right and passes the isolated hostel.

 2

Soon after passing the youth hostel the valley floor is met and you should remain on the main track as it begins to climb. Ignore a right fork and soon pass under an ornate bridge. Now continue on the main track for 1 mile to reach the driveway to **Polseden Lacey**. Cross the drive and turn left on a grassy strip that remains parallel to the drive.

 3

When the drive bends left remain ahead on an unmade track. In 130 yards at a fork, ignore a byway ahead and go left along the track signposted to **Yew Tree Farm**. As the

Drive and Stroll

track reaches the tarmac drive beside the entrance gate to **Home Farm House** keep ahead on the drive as it goes down hill and passes under two footbridges. 30 yards after passing under the second bridge ignore the drive as it bends left and go ahead on a raised bridleway lined by yew trees.

At the top of a rise, the bridleway meets with a T-junction. Turn right here and pass the entrance of **Yew Tree Farm** where in 5 yards you should keep left at a fork and pass under power cables. As you press on along this cart track a well-placed seat to your left offers a fine view of **Polesden Lacey** house. Now remain on this wonderful cart track as it enters the depths of fine woodland.

There has been a succession of fine houses over the centuries at Polesden Lacey with the present one being built from a Thomas Cubitt design for Joseph Bonsor in the 1820s. The biggest influence on

A seat well-placed to enjoy the view

the house, however, is from the sumptuous furnishings installed by the Hon. Mrs Greville, a society hostess who lived here from 1906. On her death in 1942 she very generously left its entirety to the National Trust.

After 1 mile of easy walking the track brings you back to the road at **Ranmore**. Turn left alongside the road on the wildflower speckled grassy strip to rejoin the car park and to complete this splendid stroll.

Place of Interest Nearby

Denbies Wine Estate in the Mole Valley is the largest vineyard in England. Vineyard tours show each stage of winemaking while the visitor centre includes a wine-tasting cellar, wine bar and restaurant for light lunches and refreshments. Open daily January to March 10am to 4.30pm (Sunday 11.30am to 5.30pm) and April to December daily from 10am to 5.30pm (Sunday 10.30am to 5.30pm). Off the A24 London Road, ¼ mile north of Dorking. Telephone: 01306 876616.

14 Around Ockley

A cottage by the village green at Ockley

The Walk 3½ miles **Terrain** Fairly level
Map OS Landranger 187 Dorking, Reigate & Crawley (GR 148402)

How to get there

Ockley is 8 miles south of Dorking on the A29. **Parking**: A small parking area is beside the A29 and opposite the Inn On The Green. Additional parking may be found by the cricket pitch at the southern end of the green.

Drive and Stroll

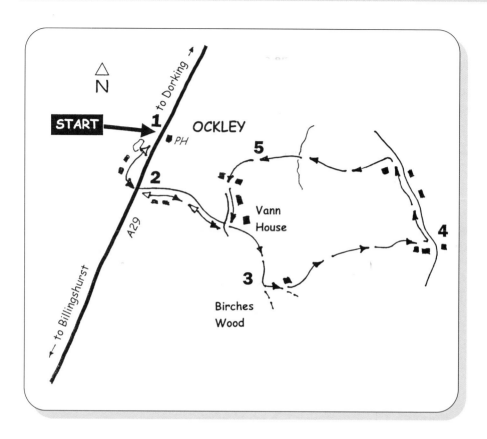

Introduction

This easy stroll starts from beside Ockley's glorious village green where pretty rose-bowered cottages and lily-covered village pond are passed. After circumnavigating a cricket pitch, the way crosses the A29 coast road and continues along Friday Street, a quiet country lane with an unusual name. After meeting the gates of Vann House the route follows a bridleway into a shallow valley where it passes through the peaceful wooded area of Vann Lake Nature Reserve and crosses a woodland stream.

Soon a driveway is met that offers easy walking as the circuit climbs out of the valley to meet a country lane by a quiet grouping of cottages alongside Stylehurst Farm. Turning north along the lane the route passes some substantial houses set well back in the trees before continuing on an easy-to-follow path that has fine viewpoints across pleasant fields to the heights of Leith Hill and its lofty tower.

The Inn On The Green

There was a time when the name of an inn would last for centuries and even bus routes became known by them, but modern marketing methods demand that changes be made and so what was the Red Lion has now become the Inn On The Green. A change of name maybe but you cannot hide the inn's 16th-century origins. It is cosy and comfortable with a good selection of home-cooked food from an ever-changing menu that suits all tastes, from simple bar snacks to something more substantial like rump steak with all the trimmings. Telephone: 01306 711032.

The Old Bakery and Post Office simple take-away sandwiches, tea, coffee and cold drinks are available from the village store just yards from the parking area.

THE WALK

The straightness of the A29 here through Ockley is because it follows the exact line of the Roman-built Stane Street, which linked Chichester to London.

From the parking area, cross the village green to meet a dirt track by a couple of pretty cottages. Now turn left to soon reach the village pond where you should continue ahead alongside its left bank to meet another dusty track. Remain on the track as it first passes a football pitch and continues around the boundary of a cricket pitch to end at the **A29**.

The Battle of Ockley was fought here in 851AD when an army of West Saxons met an invading Danish army heading south from the Thames. The Anglo-Saxon Chronicle reported that the Danes were so heavily defeated that none were left to bury the dead.

Cross the A29 with caution as the traffic travels far too fast here, and continue ahead along **Friday Street**. After passing several houses, continue ahead through a gateway marked as private, the driveway is in fact a bridleway. When the ornate gates of **Vann House** are met, continue ahead on a signed bridleway just to their right. The fenced bridleway first skirts a garden before descending gently into a shallow valley where it meets with **Vann Lake Nature Reserve**. Ignore side paths and press on along the bridleway to meet a fork by a low directional post. Fork left here and cross a wooden bridge over a stream.

Continue up a low rise to a second fork in the path. Here go left to soon pass a house and to join its driveway. Press on ahead along the drive that soon becomes **Vann Lake Road**, a quiet backwater that serves no more than a dozen houses. The road finally ends at a T-junction with **Weare Street** by a small cluster of houses and **Stylehurst Farm**.

Ockley's glorious village green

The way is now to the left along **Weare Street** where you will pass a few exclusive houses that would be idyllic, if it were not for the Gatwick flight path. Soon after passing **Woodland Drive** on your right, ignore a footpath on your right, but 20 yards later turn left on a signed footpath beside the entrance to an unseen house named **Weavers**. Now follow this path as it first skirts a garden before continuing through woodland and beside scenic fields with fine views to **Leith Hill**. Almost un-noticed the footpath is joined by a bridleway and together they continue ahead over a stream and along a ribbon of trees to reach a field gate.

Go through the gate and cross the field to meet a wooden electricity pole from where you should bear slightly left to meet and cross a stile. Continue between the buildings of **Vann Farm** and a cottage to reach a tarmac drive which you should follow until it brings back to the gates of **Vann House**. From here turn right along **Friday Street** and re-trace your steps back to **Ockley** village green and the end of this super stroll.

Place of Interest Nearby

Dorking and District Museum displays collections with a strong local influence that include farming and domestic items, and even a 3-metre long fossil of an iguanodon tailbone. Open Wednesday and Thursday from 2pm to 5pm and Saturday from 10am until 4pm. The Old Foundry, 62 West Street, Dorking. Telephone: 01306 876591.

15 Around Banstead Heath

A picnic table in the shade of pines

The Walk 4 miles **Terrain** Gently undulating downland
Map OS Landranger 187 Dorking, Reigate & Crawley (GR 237556)

How to get there

Tadworth is 3 miles north of junction 8 of the M25. From the Tadworth roundabout on the A217, take the B2032 signed to Headley. **Parking**: 50 yards after passing the Blue Anchor public house turn hard left into Mill Road and park on the right-hand side after 100 yards.

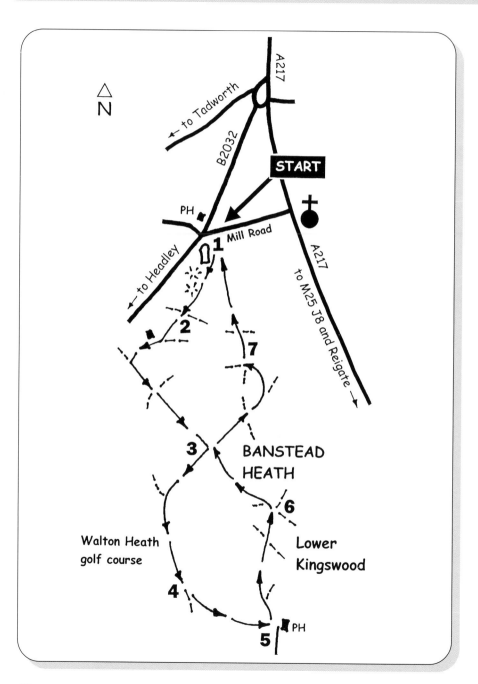

Introduction

This glorious stroll across a heathland plateau some 600 feet above sea level offers fine panoramas over the surrounding downland. With plenty of picnic spots and the absence of roads and farm animals, the route is ideal for children to run around to their hearts' content. Starting by Tadworth Mill, the way soon passes by ancient earthworks before crossing open downland to reach woodland and Banstead Heath proper beyond.

With the constant accompaniment of skylarks above, the way continues along wide grassy paths and passes by Walton Heath golf course to reach the Sportsman public house at Lower Kingswood and the halfway point of the circuit. The return continues along more pleasant paths that skirt the open downs before rejoining the dappled shade of woodland and all too soon crossing a large meadow to meet up with the old mill and the end of this enjoyable circuit.

The Sportsman

Said once to have been a hunting lodge for royalty and dating back to 1500, this fine old pub has built itself a good reputation for its food and ales. Ideally situated at the halfway point of this circuit it makes a handy place to take on refreshment, although facing Banstead Heath can make it rather popular on summer weekends. Morning coffee from 10am and a good selection of typical pub food from open sandwiches and a ploughman's to a main menu that includes a roasted vegetable lasagne with a side salad at lunchtime. Not necessary to book for cooked food but advisable during busy summer weekends. Telephone: 01737 246655.

THE WALK

From **Mill Road**, pass through a ribbon of trees on the south side to meet a large grassy meadow. Go ahead alongside the boundary hedge of a well-sited house and soon pass by **Tadworth Mill** seen in a garden on your right.

When the mill was first built is not recorded, but by the late 19th-century two of its sails had fallen off and it was being powered by a small stationary engine. The mill finally ceased working in 1902 and lost its two remaining sails 20 years later. During 1941 it was damaged by a German bomb and 3 years later by a flying bomb. The fact that it has survived a rather chequered history is a tribute to its builder!

Continue ahead alongside birch trees that mask earthworks, which are believed to be the remains of **medieval cattle enclosures**.

Drive and Stroll

At the end of these birch trees continue ahead over a crossing path and when the path descends keep right as it divides. With a house in view to your right, continue down a dip to the bottom corner. Press on half right now along a wide bridleway with a garden on your right. Soon ignore a path to your left, but 40 yards later, at a T-junction by a finger post, turn left along a bridleway signed to **Lower Kingswood**. Ignore side paths and continue on this wide track which, after leaving woodland, is lined with birch and gorse. Finally the track ends at a junction of paths with open downland ahead of you.

Turn right here along a wide, straight grassy horse-ride that skirts open downland to your left. Ignore side paths and follow the ride leftwards when it nears **Walton Heath golf course**. Keep to the well-used ride as it traces the edge of the golf course and pass by a couple of coal duty posts.

Coal duty posts marked the boundary around London where tax on coal entering the capital became due. The tax was originally introduced to help re-build London after the great fire in 1666 and although it ceased in 1889, many of these early-Victorian cast-iron posts are still found in Surrey. The inscription '24 & 25 VICT CAP 42'

refers to chapter 42 of the statute book during the 24th and 25th years of Queen Victoria's reign under which the posts were erected. Many posts were cast before the act came into force and therefore have had the first 2 and the T of VICT ground off to facilitate a correction plate that added the word ACT. Most of the posts are Grade II listed.

When the ride swings right at the end of the golf course, maintain your direction ahead. With two indistinct tracks ahead of you take the left-hand one and press on towards a gap in the trees ahead of you. Ignore a crossing path to soon reach a vehicle barrier with **The Sportsman** public house beyond.

The way now turns leftwards from this barrier as the route begins the homeward journey. Follow a hard surfaced path and when this soon ends, ignore a path on your right that enters woodland. Continue ahead along a horse ride that stays close to woodland and with open heath to your left. Remain ahead over a narrow crossing path and continue on the dip slope until a larger junction of tracks is met.

6

Here, go left on a bridleway signed to **Dorking Road**. In 20 yards ignore a left fork and remain on the main track and again at a second fork. The bridleway passes through a ribbon of woodland and after climbing out of a dip it re-joins a junction of tracks we met earlier. Now turn right along the wide horse-ride and at a junction of tracks by a barrier, go ahead. After 120 yards, fork left on the main track that soon rounds a bend to reach another barrier.

Coal duty post on Banstead Heath

 (7)

Turn right here down a stony path and pass through a dip to reach a junction of paths. Go ahead on the upward slope and remain close to trees on your right. Keep ahead over a crossing path and soon pass through a ribbon of birch trees to re-join the large meadow. Remain ahead now towards **Tadworth Mill** and very soon you will find yourself at the end of this exhilarating stroll.

Place of Interest Nearby

6 miles south along the A217 and the other side of the M25 is Reigate, a town that boasts two caves; **Baron's Cave** is one of the oldest show caves in England while **Tunnel Cave** is part of a huge sand cave system. Open on selected days each year. Telephone: 01737 823456.

16 Reigate Heath and Buckland

Buckland pond and tithe barn

The Walk 4½ miles **Terrain** Level tracks and field paths
Map OS Landranger 187 Dorking, Reigate & Crawley (GR 239502)

How to get there

From Reigate town centre take the A25 east towards Dorking. Flanchford Road is on your left by an open area after 1 mile. **Parking**: There are free car parks in Flanchford Road.

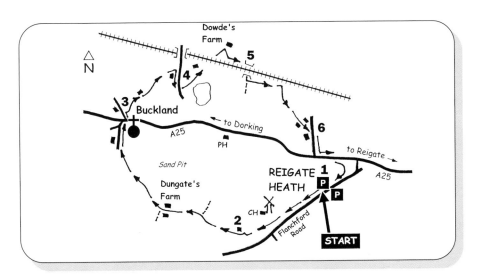

Introduction

This easy stroll below the Buckland Hills passes over Reigate Heath by its well-preserved windmill that, since 1862, has been given over to church services. The circuit continues through pleasant fields to reach Dungate's Farm and by following the farm drive into the centre of Buckland the way takes you past Yewdells, a lovely Grade II listed house with a unique feature in its garden.

After passing by Buckland's pretty church, tithe barn, Street Farm and a 16th-century cottage that once served as a brew-house, the route crosses fields with a backdrop of the Buckland Hills. All too soon the way turns back and rejoins Reigate Heath where it passes by a cricket and football pitch to reach Flanchford Road and the end of this super stroll. There are three stiles on the route that are difficult to negotiate if you are accompanied by a medium to large sized dog.

The Jolly Farmers

You will find the Jolly Farmers pub half a mile west along the A25 from the Flanchford Road junction. The welcoming pub was, I have been reliably informed, the site of a detachment from a searchlight regiment stationed here during the Battle of Britain. Their HQ was a private room at the rear where liquid nutrition was supplied through a small window to the bar – not a bad posting I hear you say. With long opening and serving hours all tastes are catered for, from the humble sandwich (until 5pm) to a fillet steak with brandy and paprika sauce. No need to book. Telephone: 01737 221355.

Drive and Stroll

THE WALK

When approaching the parking areas from the **Reigate** direction, the stroll starts from the far end of the right-hand area. Follow a sandy bridleway that remains parallel to **Flanchford Road**. When opposite **Bonny's Road** remain on the bridleway as it zigzags before continuing to shadow the road. At the driveway to the golf clubhouse go right for 5 yards before turning left and continuing on a downhill path that brings you to a fairway.

Paying due attention to flying golf balls, cross the fairway to a house in the trees opposite and press on along a wide path to its left. Continue through fields on a well-trodden path until a fork is met alongside the **Shag Brook**. Go left here to reach **Dungate's Farm**, once a working farm, but now with its fields lost to a huge quarry the house has been gentrified and the barns given over to equestrian needs. Keep ahead between the farm buildings and press on along the lane where you will later pass a house named **Yewdells** on your left.

In the garden of Yewdells is England's last surviving wind-powered sawmill. The Grade II listed house dates from the early 18th-century and has been the home for generations of carpenters with the site remaining registered as a sawmill until 1950. Now also Grade II listed, the mill is thought to date from around 1860 and has undergone extensive restoration of late.

Press on along the lane to reach **Buckland's village shop** and the centre of this small hamlet.

Cross the **A25** with caution and continue ahead on a path between the tithe barn and picturesque pond.

By the pond is 17th-century Street Farm, disguising its age well under a covering of plaster. Its tithe barn has been converted to a handsome residence, as has the nearby village school that was designed by Henry Woodyer in 1862. Containing two classrooms – one for infants and the other for children up to 14 years of age, the school served my mother and two aunts well when, as children in the 1930s, they lived at Dungate's Farm.

Pass **Street Farmhouse** and then turn right into **Slough Lane** by the old school. At the end of the lane by the gateway of **Slough House**, fork right through a gate and continue on a signed path along a field edge to reach a stile opposite. Press on through a small paddock to reach a lane beside a house.

Reigate Heath and the church–windmill

 (4)

Turn right along the lane and 50 yards before a left bend by power lines, cross a stile on your left. Now go diagonally half left to meet a hedgerow at a protruding corner of the field. Keep to the right-hand field edge until opposite an old house. Now maintain direction over the field and cross a stile ahead of you at a railway line. Take note of the *stop, look and listen* sign and go over the railway and a stile ahead and cross a small paddock to a field gate. Do not go through the gate. Turn right and now follow the edge of the paddock back to a stile beside the railway embankment. Cross the stile and continue left alongside the embankment to reach a further stile.

 (5)

Turn right and go under a bridge and cross a stile in 8 yards to your left. Go left up a slope and continue on a fenced path that remains parallel to the railway track. At a stile the path now turns right and with the railway track at your back, follow a field edge towards a stile with a house beyond. Go ahead to

the left of the house and press on along a path beside a brick wall. Follow this path as it continues between and, unusually, through a couple of gardens to finally meet a road.

 (6)

Turn right along the road to soon reach the **A25**. Turn left here along the pavement until you reach **Colley Manor Drive**. Now cross the **A25** with care and turn left along a bridleway and at a football and cricket pitch, turn right alongside woodland to very soon reach **Flanchford Road** where, upon turning right, you will rejoin the parking area and the end to this good circuit.

Place of Interest Nearby

Reigate Priory Museum is housed in a Grade I listed building set in over 60 acres of parkland and lake. There is a gift shop and an ever-changing exhibition. Open each Wednesday and Saturday from 2pm to 4.30pm from Easter to early December during term time. Bell Street, Reigate. Telephone: 01737 222550 (afternoons).

17 | Around Happy Valley

The church of St Peter and St Paul on the outskirts of Chaldon

The Walk 3¼ miles **Terrain** Undulating downland
Map OS Landranger (GR 317568)

How to get there

From the A23 Brighton Road 1 mile south of Purley, turn into Stoats Nest Road (B2030) signed to Old Coulsdon. When the open area of Coulsdon Common is reached after 2 miles, turn right into Fox Lane by a bus stop. **Parking**: The large Happy Valley car parking area is at the end of the lane.

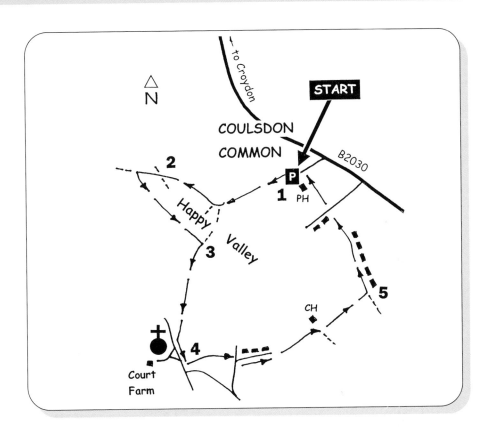

Introduction

This varied and interesting stroll leads you first around the flower-filled grassland of Happy Valley, a wonderful wildlife area that strangely is owned by the City of London. Undulating paths then lead across arable fields to meet up with the Church of St Peter and St Paul on the outskirts of Chaldon where inside on the west wall is a large 12th-century red ochre painting of the Last Judgement.

After leaving the coolness of the church the way follows a pleasant path across a field to meet a quiet residential road from where the route continues through a valley to meet a path that runs along the edge of what was once Caterham Army Barracks. The barracks have made way for an interesting housing development where some of the former buildings have been converted to pleasant homes. From here a short path through woodland completes the stroll. Part of the circuit is on heavy clay soil and is best left for the drier summer months.

Drive and Stroll

The Fox

To reach the parking area you pass by the Fox public house where the signage boasts 'great British food all day every day'. An explanation for its position so far back from the road is given by old maps that show a drovers' road passing close to its door. The Fox is a comfortable pub with a good range of snacks and reasonably priced hot food that will suit all tastes from the humble sandwich or soup of the day to a more substantial platter of Mediterranean vegetable lasagne. Take advantage of the seating in the garden for those warm sunny summer days where you can relax and enjoy your meal. Telephone: 01883 330401.

THE WALK

1

From the parking area continue away from **Fox Lane** on a tarmac path that runs alongside a large grassy area with a hedgerow on your right. The fittest amongst you may like to prove your prowess by tackling the obstacle course set out alongside the path. When the tarmac surface ends, press on ahead and ignore a path to your left soon after rounding a bend. Now continue on the well-defined path down the sloping hillside passing well-placed picnic seats along the way. After going through a ribbon of woodland, continue ahead to reach a junction of paths in the foot of the valley.

Growing amongst the short downland grasses here in Happy Valley are myriads of the yellow flowered cocks comb (also called yellow rattle), a partially parasitic plant. Also seen here although in much small numbers, are meadow cranesbill and the more common of our orchid species.

2

Maintain direction over crossing tracks and in 5 yards when the grassy path forks, keep to the left fork. Now press on up a slope to the top corner of the meadow to meet a finger post in the edge of woodland. Turn hard left and continue along the edge of grassland on a path signposted to **Chaldon Church** with woodland close to your right. At a second finger post continue ahead through a strip of woodland and press on along the edge of the wildflower meadow to reach a third finger post.

3

Here turn right up a slope through trees to reach a large arable field. Now follow a well-used path through this and a second field to finally reach a small lane. Turn left along the lane to meet a small triangle of grass. The way continues along the lane but a not-to-be-missed diversion a few yards to your right

The route through Happy Valley

brings you to **Chaldon's** unique church.

Inside, on the west wall is a most amazing painting measuring 17 feet wide by 11 feet high that grotesquely depicts the Last Judgement. The central theme shows a ladder rising to heaven with pure souls climbing up and the damned being cast into the fires of hell while all around are demons and serpents. It is believed to have been painted by a Norman monk in 1170 and was discovered under a layer of whitewash in 1870.

After your visit go back to the lane and turn right to meet a signed path in 15 yards.

  (4)

Turn left here and follow a path along a field edge and later pass beside woodland to reach a quiet lane. Turn right to meet a residential road (**Leazes Avenue**) in 15 yards where you should now turn left. When the road ends abruptly, press on ahead along a bridleway that leads you through a golf course and brings you towards the clubhouse. Swing right for a few yards here to meet a directional post where you

Drive and Stroll

ignore a footpath indicated on your right. Go ahead over a drive and continue along the bridleway where you again pass through the golf course.

 (5)

The bridleway finally reaches a T-junction with a path some 20 yards before housing is met. Here turn left along the made-up path and pass by the side of housing.

The high fence and brick wall on your right once protected Caterham's Army Barracks. Originally built in 1875 the site has given way to what is now called an 'urban village'. As you pass by here it makes for an interesting diversion to see how well some of the old barrack buildings have been integrated into the scheme.

Happy Valley

Continue along this straight path – a remnant of an old drovers' road to meet a residential road. Go ahead through a gate opposite and press on through woodland to soon pass the **Fox** pub to reach **Fox Lane** where this interesting stroll ends.

Place of Interest Nearby

East Surrey Museum contains geological and archaeological displays as well as crafts and other changing exhibitions. Open Wednesdays and Saturdays between 10am and 5pm and Sundays from 2pm to 5pm. Stafford Road, Caterham. Telephone: 01883 340275.

18 Around Outwood

Looking towards the North Downs

The Walk 4¼ miles **Terrain** Level field paths
Map OS Landranger 187 Dorking, Reigate & Crawley (GR 327456)

How to get there

Outwood is 3 miles south of Bletchingley. From the A25 crossroads near Bletchingley's church, go south along Outwood Lane until the windmill is reached. **Parking**: Turn right opposite the mill on a rough track and park in the National Trust car park on the common.

Drive and Stroll

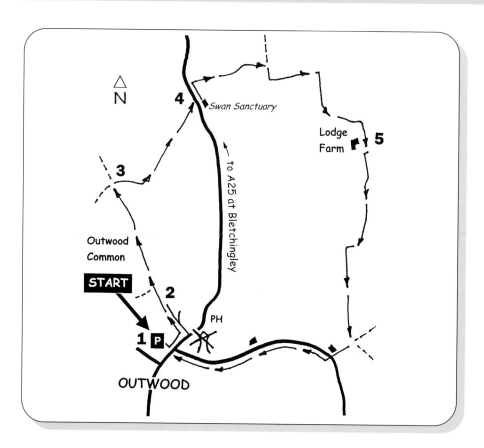

Introduction

What a joy and a pleasure this easy-to-follow circuit is. For almost the whole of its route it passes through scenic fields with expansive views over the peaceful Surrey landscape. After leaving Outwood Common and its ancient windmill behind, the way follows field paths lined with springtime wildflowers and all the while there are fine views across to the North Downs. After passing Outwood Swan Sanctuary the route follows pleasant cart tracks and brings you to the buildings of 18th-century Lodge Farm.

From here, the circuit turns south towards Outwood on another wonderful cart track that offers easy walking beside fields where skylarks sing out their song overhead. During spring the May blossom in the hedgerows exudes its strong heady perfume on the breeze and yet again there are fine distant views. Finally the route follows a country lane, which brings you back to Outwood's fine windmill and the end of this great stroll.

The Bell Inn

The Bell Inn at Outwood has an enviable position sitting as it does so near the famous mill that draws people from far and wide. Without much competition you could think that it would lead to some complacency, but not a bit of it, the food and service are top class. During the summer months a barbecue in the garden sizzles with fresh fish, meats and vegetarian fare while in the restaurant a more refined selection includes a pan-fried salmon dish marinated in sweet ginger. Watch out though if you wish to eat in the restaurant, as booking is essential on summer weekends and Bank Holidays. Telephone: 01342 842989.

THE WALK

Outwood Mill is England's oldest working windmill and dates back to 1665, just one year before the Great Fire of London. It is said that from its roof the people of Outwood watched the flames consuming London some 22 miles to the north. During 1870 a second, and larger octagonal smock mill was erected on the site but failed to see off the old mill. By the 1930s, the smock mill had lost two of its sails and had fallen into disuse with its final indignity coming during the early 1960s when it collapsed during a storm.

 1

From the car park head back towards the road and after a few yards turn left over a small piece of grass to meet a narrow lane. Turn left along the lane and pass by **The Windmill Garage**. Ignore a right fork and when the lane soon ends by a couple of cottages go ahead and cross a stile in a field edge.

 2

Press on ahead on a well-trodden path to meet a second field. Ignore a path to your left and continue ahead alongside a hedgerow as you pass through this long field to reach and cross a stile at its end.

 3

Ignoring paths to your left and ahead, turn right and continue along the top edge of this and a second field. Pass through a ribbon of trees where you cross a tiny brook to meet another field. The way is now diagonally left through this field to meet and cross a stile in the hedgerow. Now maintain direction over two more fields to finally meet **Outwood Lane** by the **Outwood Swan Sanctuary**.

 4

Turn left along the lane and as it soon bends to the right, go right on a signed bridleway along a cart track. After passing alongside woodland the track meets a T-junction. Turn right here and follow

Drive and Stroll

Outwood Common and the windmill

the bridleway along the cart track as it zigzags beside fields and brings you to the concrete driveway of **Lodge Farm**.

  (5)

Continuing on the bridleway, keep ahead over the drive and go through a gate. Pass between a field and farm buildings to reach a second gate and a cart track. Now turn left along the track and remain on it until it finally ends in woodland at a T-junction. Turn right along a bridleway to soon reach **Gayhouse Lane** beside a house named **Hornecourt Cottage**. Turn right along the lane where you later pass 17th-century **Gay House** before rejoining **Outwood Mill** and bringing this pretty circuit to an end.

Place of Interest Nearby

Outwood Mill has a small museum while ducks, geese and sheep run free in the grounds. There is also a small children's play area. Open on Sundays and Bank Holidays from Easter to September between 2pm and 6pm. Telephone: 01342 843458.

19 Godstone and Bletchingley

Garston Park

The Walk 5¼ miles **Terrain** Fairly level with two hills
Map OS Landranger 187 Dorking, Reigate & Crawley (GR 350515)

How to get there

Godstone is on the A25 and ¾ mile south of junction 6 of the M25.
Parking: The car park is by Godstone's village pond and green a few
yards south of the small one-way system.

Drive and Stroll

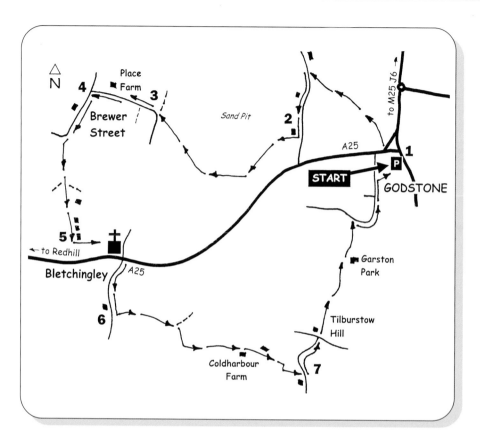

Introduction

This glorious stroll has plenty to interest all; scenic field paths, ancient farms and houses, and the magnificent rolling parkland of Garston Park. After leaving Godstone's pretty village pond and green behind, the way passes through level fields and brings you to the small hamlet of Brewer Street where old buildings abound. From this lovely little place a rising path brings you to Bletchingley's St Mary's church by the High Street where plenty of refreshment may be found.

Leaving Bletchingley behind, the route then follows a section of the Greensand Way long-distance path from where there are fantastic views over the weald as far as the South Downs. As the route turns towards Godstone there is a short climb up Tilburstow Hill to reach the scenic fields of Garston Park which bring you back to the outskirts of Godstone from where it is just a short stroll to the village green and the end of the superb circuit.

The Hare and Hounds

There is no shortage of pubs and eateries around Godstone so you have plenty to choose from and talking of choice, try the menu at the Hare and Hounds at the northern end of the village green. There is something for everyone; burgers, ploughman's, sandwiches, baguettes, toasties and main courses that include anything from pan-fried calf's liver to seafood tagliatelle provençal and Thai chicken curry. No need to book. Telephone: 01883 742296.

THE WALK

From the village green, go to its northeastern corner to meet **Bletchingley Road**. Cross the road and continue ahead on a footpath between a cottage and the **Hare & Hounds** pub. After 100 yards go through a kissing gate on your left and bear left across a meadow. Pass through a second kissing gate and continue on a fenced path to reach and cross a stile at field edge. Go diagonally half left over the field and aim to the left of farm buildings to reach and cross a stile in a hedgerow to meet a lane.

Turn left along the lane and soon after passing the entrance to **North Park Farm Quarry** ignore a footpath on your left and turn right on a wide bridleway beside number **1 North Park Cottage**. In 150 yards when a gate bars your way, bear left and follow a sandy bridleway between fields until it finally meets a junction of tracks with a gate and a road a few yards to your left.

Keep ahead on the bridleway that remains parallel to the road. When the bridleway turns abruptly right, go left to join the road and maintain your direction ahead. After going over a small rise you pass by the driveway to **Place Farm House** and soon you will meet a T-junction.

Closer inspection of 18th-century Place Farm House reveals a fragment of the much earlier Bletchingley Place within the front wall. Anne of Cleves, the fourth wife of Henry VIII lived here after their divorce in 1540.

At this T-junction turn left along **Brewer Street** and soon pass magnificent **Brewerstreet Farmhouse**. Soon you will pass by **6 Brewer Street**, a 16th-century building that until recent times was three cottages, while in a past life it was **The Brew House** after which this hamlet was named. When the road bends sharply right maintain direction ahead on a grassy path that rises slowly and leaves the

Brewerstreet Farmhouse dates back to the 15th century

hamlet behind. Ignore side paths and remain ahead as you meet a drive.

⤶ (5)

When finally an industrial building is reached at a small junction of lanes, turn left alongside the building and keep ahead on a pretty footpath until reaching the graveyard of **St Mary's church**. Fork right through the graveyard to meet **Bletchingley High Street** and cross to the **Whyte Harte** pub before turning left to meet a crossroads by the **Prince Albert** pub – no shortage of refreshment here. Turn right along **Outwood Lane** and continue alongside the road

until 50 yards after passing **The Rectory** you should turn left on a signed bridleway by a gate.

⤶ (6)

Pass by a small pond and ignore the occasional side path. When the bridleway divides follow the right fork between fields and at the foot of a slope ignore a track to your left. The route follows the **Greensand Way** ahead between banks and for sometime it remains on the edge of woodland with fantastic views over the **Weald** to your right. Finally the path meets with a lane and here you should continue ahead along the lane. Remain ahead on the

Greensand Way when the lane bends to the left and pass by a couple of wonderfully sited cottages. Continue on the path as it zigzags alongside a field and ends at a road.

Turn left along the road, which now climbs **Tilburstow Hill** to soon reach a T-junction. Go ahead on a path opposite and cross a stile to soon meet another. Cross this and follow the waymarked path until it reaches a driveway. Go ahead along the drive and when it divides follow the left-hand fork until it ends at a lane. Turn right and continue along **Ivy**

Mill Lane until after passing **Godstone village school** you should turn right over the green to end this exhilarating stroll.

Along this quiet lane you will pass Ivy Mill House, which dates back to 1698. Opposite are the ruins of Ivy Mill, a watermill that suffered a disaster one day in 1909 when heavy rain caused the bank to burst and the millpond to drain. After repairs the mill continued to work until 1922 when it finally closed. Two years later it was destroyed by fire and only the footings remain.

Place of Interest Nearby

The British Wildlife Centre on the A22 between Blindley Heath and Newchapel 5 miles south of Godstone was created from a working dairy farm where now indigenous wild animals in enclosures that reflect their natural habitat have replaced the cows. There is a coffee shop, picnic area and a small museum. Open 10am to 5pm from April to October on Sundays and Bank Holidays and every day during school half term and summer holidays. Telephone: 01342 834658.

20 | Blindley Heath and Crowhurst

A shady picnic spot

The Walk 4¾ miles **Terrain** Level
Map OS Landranger 187 Dorking, Reigate & Crawley (GR 364451)

How to get there

Blindley Heath is on the A22 and 5 miles south of junction 6 of the M25.
Parking: Turn into Ray Lane at Blindley Heath traffic lights signposted to Lingfield and in 50 yards go right into a small car park by the cricket pitch and village pond.

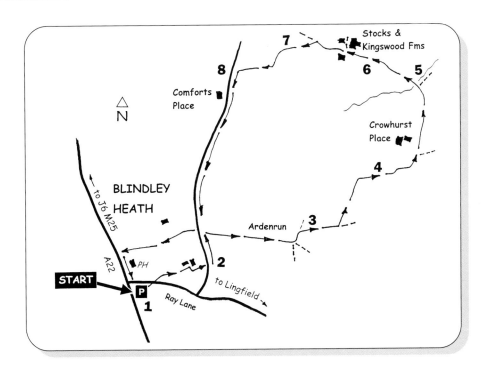

Introduction

This easy-to-follow stroll is not as it seems from its title, for instead of pine covered heath, the route follows glorious field paths through scenic farmland where the views are far reaching. Starting off beside the village pond, which itself makes a pretty picnic spot, the route heads for Ardenrun, once the home of a wealthy playboy and now a large showground.

After leaving the showground the circuit makes its way along wonderful field paths with great views and passes 15th-century Crowhurst Place. Continuing through peaceful meadows the way begins to swing westward to reach a country lane that is followed for some time before meeting a path that crosses more meadows and brings you to the A22 beside the popular Blue Anchor public house and its large garden. From here it is just a couple of hundred yards back to the cricket pitch and the end of this very pleasant stroll.

The Blue Anchor

The friendly staff offer the cheeriest of welcomes at this most enjoyable pub. Inside there are low beams, an inglenook fireplace and bags of character.

Drive and Stroll

During the warmer summer months you may choose to sit at a table in the garden but if you pass this way during the cold winter months, a glowing log fire in the bar will warm you through and through. The last time I visited I treated myself to a Mediterranean vegetable lasagne dish which came with salad leaves and delicious seasoned chips, while my wife was surprised to find her tuna, sweet corn and spring onion sandwich came in a rustic roll and was also accompanied by a pile of seasoned chips – great value but not so good for dieters. No need to book. Telephone: 01342 830001.

THE WALK

From the car park turn right along **Ray Lane** for 100 yards before crossing the road to meet a track to the right of a house with a very wide frontage. Follow the track for 40 yards before turning right on a signed footpath that goes through mature oak woodland. Soon cross a stile and keep ahead on a fenced path between paddocks. Continue through a field gate and alongside a large barn to reach the buildings of an equestrian centre. Go right here and pass the end of **stable block C** before turning left and continuing along a drive where you pass through ornate gates and meet a country lane.

Now turn left and continue along the lane until you reach the gateway and drive signed **Ardenrun** on your right. Turn right here and continue along the long straight drive with large fields to your right that make up the **Ardenrun Showground**. Remain on the drive as it finally bends left and crosses a stream.

Ardenrun Place was the home of Woolf Barnato, a fabulously rich young man who, during the 1920s, provided the finance for the then ailing Bentley Motors. With his finance and driving skills, the legend of the great green Bentleys and the 'Bentley Boys' took off. He won Le Mans three years in a row plus prestigious races at Brooklands in 1929 and 1930. His wealth came from South African diamonds and his parties at Ardenrun became legendary. Sadly the house burnt down in 1933.

When the drive divides by a wonderful stone barn, turn right along a cart track. 20 yards after the well-used cart track turns right into a field, cross a stile on your left. Continue along the left-hand field edge to reach and cross a stile in the top corner of the field. Press on ahead over the next field to meet a marker post by a hedgerow. Now turn right alongside the hedgerow to meet and cross a stile under trees.

Remain ahead and continue along the field edge and at its end go left through a kissing gate. Maintain your original direction now along an avenue of newly planted trees at the end of which the path swings leftwards. Continue between mature oak trees and ignore a signed footpath on your right. Remain ahead on a path marked as the **Lingfield and Crowhurst Age to Age Walk**. By keeping ahead now the driveway to **Crowhurst Place** is reached. Continue over the drive and press on along the right side of a field with expansive views. A look over your shoulder here also gives you a view of **Crowhurst Place**.

Crowhurst Place dates from 1425 and was originally a wealthy yeoman's moated manor house. In 1918 it underwent a transformation with the addition of a new wing and a heavy restoration programme that now hides the oldest parts. The brick dovecot dates from 1918, as does the gatehouse at the end of the drive.

 5

At the end of this field continue ahead to meet the corner of a second field by an oak tree and a junction of paths. Here cross a small bridge over a stream and ignore a path to your right. The way continues over a field towards low barns behind a hedgerow where you meet a junction of farm tracks. As you cross this field the spire of **Crowhurst church** will be seen to your right.

Beside Crowhurst church is a huge yew tree thought to be 4,000 years old. In 1820 villagers hollowed out the trunk and found a cannonball from the civil war embedded in the wood. The tree became a Victorian curiosity when a table and benches large enough to seat a dozen people were installed.

 6

At the corner of this field, ignore farm tracks to left and right and press on ahead along the central track. After passing cottages continue ahead between posts and ignore a signed path to your right. Go ahead between barns to reach a gate and a tarmac drive. Pass through the gate and continue along the tarmac drive and pass through a second gate. 40 yards after passing the gateway of **Stocks Farm**, turn left over a stile to enter a small paddock. In another 40 yards go through a field gate on the right and cross a large field to meet and cross a stile in the far corner.

 7

Turn right after 5 yards over a concrete bridge and cross a second stile. Now turn left along the field edge and cross a stile ahead of you in the hedgerow. Turn right now to meet another in 40 yards where you remain ahead to finally cross a stile beside cottages and meet a country lane.

 8

If you are walking with children it is

Drive and Stroll

The straight drive beside the Ardenrun showground

best to keep them in check here because of the passing traffic. Turn left along the lane and remain on it for almost ¾ mile. About 50 yards before reaching the gateway to **Ardenrun**, turn right along a driveway signed as a footpath and when it bends right into **Heath Grange**, keep ahead on a fenced path. Cross a stile and maintain direction through a meadow and cross a second stile. Pass through an archway of sloe bushes to reach a tarmac path and continue ahead beside the **Blue Anchor** pub to reach the **A22**. Turn left here to soon reach **Ray Lane** and the end of this easy and interesting circuit.

Place of Interest Nearby

Haxted Watermill Museum is 3 miles east of Blindley Heath. Open from April to September on Wednesdays, weekends and Bank Holidays from 1pm to 5pm. Follow Ray Lane east for 1¼ miles and turn left as directed at Lingfield Common. Telephone: 01732 862914.